A QUICK C   N

WORD 6

For Windows

*
*
*
*
*
*

STEVE LAMBERT

JOYCE COX

AN ONLINE PRESS B

PUBLISHED BY
Online Press Incorporated
14320 NE 21st Street, Suite 18
Bellevue, WA 98007
Phone: (206) 641-3434, (800) 854-3344
Fax: (206) 641-4728
Email: QCbooksOnlinePress@msn.com
Web site: http://www.qkcourse.com

Publisher's Cataloging in Publication
(Prepared by Quality Books Inc.)

Lambert, Steve.
    A quick course in Word 6 for Windows / Steve Lambert, Joyce Cox.

    p. cm.
    ISBN 1-879399-27-X

    1. Microsoft Word for Windows.   2. Word processing.   I. Cox, Joyce.   II. Title.

Z52.5.M523L34 1993   652.5'536
                         QBI93-21966
                                 93-086381
                                 CIP

Printed and bound in the United States of America

   3 4 5 6 7 8 9 W O R D 3 2 1 0

Other Quick Course® books
Don't miss our other Quick Course® titles! Call us at 1-800-854-3344

*A Quick Course in Windows 95 • A Quick Course in Windows 3.1 • A Quick Course in Windows for
Workgroups • A Quick Course in DOS • A Quick Course in Microsoft Office for Windows 95
A Quick Course in Microsoft Office for Windows • A Quick Course in Excel for Windows
A Quick Course in PowerPoint for Windows • A Quick Course in Microsoft Works for Windows
A Quick Course in Lotus 1-2-3 for Windows • A Quick Course in WordPerfect for Windows*
Plus more!

Contents

1

Word Basics:
Writing a Letter

What you will learn...

December 10, 1993

Amy Meadows, President
EarthWare Inc.
4293 East Willows Avenue
Redmond, WA 98052

<u>RE: 1993 CARSON AWARDS</u>

Dear Ms. Meadows:

I am pleased to be the bearer of good news! Yesterday the Carson Committee voted unanimously to present its *1993 Packaging Innovation Award* to your company, EarthWare Inc. Your experiments during the past year with popcorn, peanut shells, and recycled cardboard are an impressive demonstration of EarthWare's ongoing commitment to the environment.

As you know, the prestigious Carson Awards recognize companies who actively work to ensure that their business practices are environmentally sensitive. This year's Packaging Innovation Award, which includes a $10,000 donation to the environmental organization of your choice, will be presented at the *Carson Gala Dinner on Friday March 18, 1994.* I will contact you next week with further details.

Again, congratulations!

Ted Lee

Most books about software programs have a chapter like this one. We tried to think of a way around it, but the fact is that if you have never used a program before, you have to get a few basics under your belt before you can do any meaningful work. You have to know how to save and retrieve files, how to enter text and move around a document with reasonable efficiency, and how to select text so that you can do something with it.

In this chapter, we cover all these topics while creating a short letter, and by the time you finish this chapter, you'll know enough to create simple documents using Word. If you have used an earlier version of Word for Windows or other word-processing programs that run under Windows, you might be able to get by with quickly scanning this chapter for new features or Word-specific techniques.

Getting Started

We assume that you've already installed both Windows and Word for Windows on your computer, and that you're ready to go. (We don't give detailed instructions for installing Word because the setup program guides you through the installation process.) We also assume that you've worked with Windows before and that you know how to use Program Manager, start programs, work with windows and icons, and so on. If you are a Windows novice, we recommend that you take a look at *A Quick Course in Windows*, another book in the Quick Course series, which will help you quickly come up to speed.

To follow the instructions in this book, you must be using a mouse. You can work with Word for Windows using only the keyboard, but for the most part, using a mouse is more efficient.

Well, let's get going. If you haven't already done so, start Word now:

1. At the DOS prompt (C:\>), type *win*, and press enter.

Starting Word for Windows

2. In Program Manager, double-click the Microsoft Word icon. (This icon appears in the Microsoft Office group window.)

When Word is loaded, you see a window containing the "Tip of the Day." Word displays a tip every time you start the program, offering useful shortcuts or hints about using various Word features. Read the tip, and then press Enter to display a blank window titled Document1, like the one shown below. We'll discuss each of the labeled elements as we use them in this chapter. (If the toolbars are not visible in your document window, display them by choosing the Toolbars command from the View menu, clicking the Standard and Formatting check boxes, and clicking OK; see page 12 if you need help choosing commands from menus. If the ruler is hidden, choose the Ruler command from the View menu. If the Word window doesn't fill your screen, click the Maximize button in the window's top-right corner.)

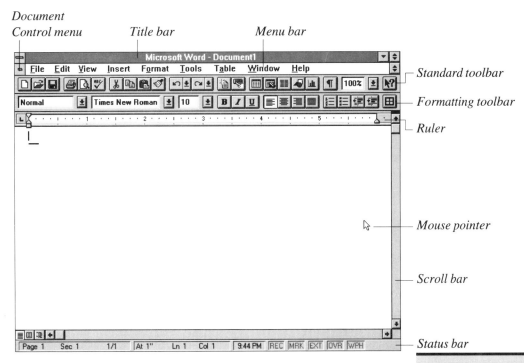

Let's start by writing the letter. (You can follow along with our example or create a document of your own.)

1. The blinking insertion point indicates where the next character you type will appear on the screen. Go ahead and type the letter shown on the next page, pressing Enter to end paragraphs and create blank lines where indicated, and pressing Backspace to erase any mistakes.

Disabling the tip of the day

To turn off the display of the tip of the day, choose Tip Of The Day from the Help menu, and in the Tip Of The Day dialog box, click the Show Tips At Startup option to deselect it, and then click OK.

December 10, 1993

Amy Meadows, President
EarthWare Inc.
4293 East Willows Avenue
Redmond, WA 98052

RE: 1993 CARSON AWARDS

Dear Ms. Meadows:

I am pleased to be the bearer of good news! Yesterday the Carson Committee voted unanimously to present its *1993 Packaging Innovation Award* to your company, EarthWare Inc. Your experiments during the past year with popcorn, peanut shells, and recycled cardboard are an impressive demonstration of EarthWare's ongoing commitment to the environment.

As you know, the prestigious Carson Awards recognize companies who actively work to ensure that their business practices are environmentally sensitive. This year's Packaging Innovation Award, which includes a $10,000 donation to the environmental organization of your choice, will be presented at the *Carson Gala Dinner on Friday March 18, 1994.* I will contact you next week with further details.

Again, congratulations!

Ted Lee

Word wrap →

As each line of text reaches the right edge of the screen, the next word you type moves to a new line. This is called *word wrapping*. Don't be concerned if the word wrapping on your screen doesn't exactly match the wrapping shown in our printout.

Now that we have some text on the screen, let's see what we can do with it.

Moving Around

You need to know how to move around a document for two reasons: so that you can view a document that is too long to fit on the screen, and so that you can edit its text.

Word wrap

When entering text, press Enter only at the ends of paragraphs, not at the ends of lines. As the text reaches the screen's right edge, the next word typed automatically wraps to a new line (hence the term word wrap). Pressing Enter ends the current paragraph and moves the insertion point to the beginning of the next line, ready to start a new paragraph.

The document window is often not big enough to display all of its contents. To bring out-of-sight information into view, you use the scroll bars. Clicking the arrow at the end of a scroll bar moves the window's contents a small distance in the direction of the arrow. Clicking on either side of a scroll box (both of which are now at the ends of their scroll bars) moves the contents one windowful. The position of the scroll box in relation to the scroll bar indicates the position of the window in relation to its contents. Drag the scroll box to see specific parts of a document; for example, the middle or end.

When it comes to editing, the insertion point is where the action is. Clicking anywhere in the text on your screen moves the insertion point to that location, or you can move the insertion point with the navigation keys, like this:

To move the insertion point...	Press...
One character left or right	Left Arrow or Right Arrow
One word left or right	Ctrl+Left Arrow or Ctrl+Right Arrow
One line up or down	Up or Down Arrow
One paragraph up or down	Ctrl+Up Arrow or Ctrl+Down Arrow
One screenful up or down	PageUp or PageDown
To first or last character on screen	Ctrl+PageUp or Ctrl+PageDown
To left or right end of current line	Home or End
To first or last character in document	Ctrl+Home or Ctrl+End

(In this book, we indicate that two or more keys are to be pressed together by separating the key names with a plus sign. For example, *press Ctrl+Home* means hold down the Ctrl key while simultaneously pressing the Home key.)

Selecting Text

Before we do anything fancy with this short document, let's discuss how to select blocks of text. Knowing how to select text efficiently saves time because you can then format all the selected text at once, instead of a letter or word at a time. The simplest way to learn how to select text is to actually do it, so follow these steps to select text blocks of different shapes and sizes using the mouse:

1. Point to any word in the document, and double-click to select the word and the following space.

2. Move the mouse pointer toward the left side of the window. When the pointer changes from an I-beam to a right-pointing arrow, it is in an area called the selection bar.

3. Position the arrow pointer in the selection bar adjacent to the line that begins *I am pleased*, and click the left mouse button once. Word highlights the line.

Clicking and double-clicking

To click something, simply move the mouse pointer over it, and then press and release a mouse button. (Unless told otherwise, use the left button.) To double-click something, move the mouse pointer over it, and then click twice rapidly. The Double Click Speed setting in the Mouse section of the Windows Control Panel controls how fast you have to double-click.

Selecting a paragraph

4. Highlight the entire first paragraph by double-clicking in the selection bar next to the paragraph.

5. Point to the end of the second paragraph, hold down the Shift key, and click the left mouse button. Word retains the existing selection and extends it to the position of the pointer.

Selecting the entire document

6. Move the pointer to the selection bar, hold down the Ctrl key, and click the left mouse button to select the entire document. (Or you can triple-click the mouse button.)

You can also drag the pointer in the selection bar to select multiple lines or paragraphs. And you can drag through the text itself to highlight exactly as much or as little as you need.

Now let's select some text with the keyboard:

1. Click an insertion point in front of the *I* in *I am pleased*.

Turning on Extend-Selection mode

2. Press the F8 key to turn on Extend-Selection mode. The letters *EXT* appear in the status bar at the bottom of the screen.

3. Press F8 again to select the word next to the insertion point. Word highlights *I* and the space following it.

4. Press F8 yet again to select the sentence containing the insertion point, like this:

Dragging to select text

To use the mouse to select a block of text, position the insertion point just to the left of the first character you want to select, press the left mouse button down, move the mouse to just past the last character you want to select, and release the mouse button. As you drag, a highlight follows the insertion point.

5. Press F8 a fourth time to select the paragraph, and a fifth time to select the entire document.

6. Now hold down the Shift key, and repeatedly press F8, shrinking the selection until only the insertion point remains. Release the Shift key.

7. Next, try pressing different Arrow keys. As long as you are in Extend-Selection mode, Word extends the selection in the direction of the key's arrow.

8. Press Esc to turn off Extend-Selection mode.

Turning off Extend-Selection mode

9. Press Home to move the insertion point to the beginning of the selection and remove the highlighting.

Giving Word Instructions

Now that you know how to select text, let's quickly cover how you tell Word what to do with the selection. You can give instructions in four ways: using buttons and lists on the toolbars; using the ruler; using menu commands; and using keyboard shortcuts.

Using the Toolbars

Word 6 for Windows comes with several predefined toolbars, each with a set of tools that are appropriate for a particular type of task. By default, the Standard and Formatting toolbars are displayed, but you can display other toolbars at any time. You can also hide all the toolbars if you need to view more of your document on the screen at one time. You'll see some of the other toolbars during the course of this book, but for now, let's take a look at the Standard and Formatting toolbars.

The Standard Toolbar

The Standard toolbar sports buttons that access the commands and utilities you will use most often as you work with Word for Windows. Throughout this book, we refer to the Standard toolbar as *the toolbar* because it is so useful that you are not likely to hide it. We won't go into a lot of detail about the buttons on the toolbar now, but by the time you finish this book, you will have used most of them. Here's how to get an idea of what each button does:

1. Move the mouse pointer to the leftmost button on the toolbar. After a few seconds, Word displays the button's name—

Whole word selection

By default, Word selects whole words. For example, if you start a selection in the middle of a word and drag beyond the last character, Word selects the entire word. If you drag to the first character of the next word, Word selects that word, and so on. You can tell Word to select only the characters you drag across by choosing Options from the Tools menu, clicking the Edit tab, clicking the Automatic Word Selection option to deselect it, and clicking OK.

in this case, New—in a box below the pointer and a brief description of the button's action in the status bar. This helpful feature is called *ToolTips*.

ToolTips

2. Move the pointer to each button in turn, pausing long enough to display its name.

Now let's see how to use one of the buttons:

Displaying nonprinting symbols

1. Move the pointer to the Show/Hide ¶ button, and click once. Word displays a ¶ wherever you pressed the Enter key and a dot wherever you pressed the Spacebar, like this:

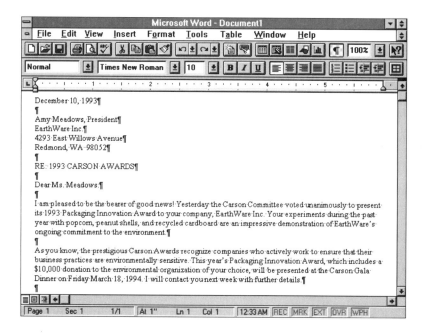

Custom toolbars

You can customize Word's toolbars by moving, removing, and adding buttons on any toolbar. Move a button by holding down the Alt key and dragging the button to its new position. (You can even drag from one toolbar to another.) Drag a copy of the button by holding down Alt+Ctrl. Remove a button by holding down Alt and dragging the button into the document window. To add a button, start by choosing Customize from the Tools menu. Select a category of actions from the Categories list to display the buttons available for that category, and then drag the button you want to the desired toolbar. To create a custom toolbar containing your favorite tools, or those you need for a specific task, choose Toolbars from the View menu, and click the New button. Assign a name in the Toolbar Name edit box, and specify which template you want to associate the toolbar with in the Make Toolbar Available To edit box. Click OK to display a new toolbar and the Customize dialog box, which you use as just described to add buttons to the custom toolbar. To delete a custom toolbar, choose Toolbars from the View menu, highlight the toolbar you want to delete, and click the Delete button (which is visible only when a custom toolbar is highlighted). You cannot undo this action. To return a toolbar to its default settings, choose Toolbars from the View menu, highlight the toolbar, and click Reset.

2. Working with these nonprinting symbols displayed is often useful, especially when you are designing complex documents. For now, however, turn off the symbols by clicking the Show/Hide ¶ button again.

The Formatting Toolbar

You use the Formatting toolbar to apply common character and paragraph formats to a text selection. *Character formats* affect the appearance of individual characters. They can be applied to any number of characters, from one to the whole document. *Paragraph formats* change characteristics such as alignment, indentation, and tab settings for entire paragraphs. You can also apply character and paragraph formats by choosing the Font and Paragraph commands from the Format menu, but clicking buttons and selecting options from the lists on the Formatting toolbar is much quicker.

Character formats

Paragraph formats

Let's see the effects produced by some of the buttons on the Formatting toolbar:

1. Move the mouse pointer into the selection bar adjacent to the subject line (*RE: 1993 CARSON AWARDS*), and then click the mouse button to select the entire line.

2. Click the Bold button on the Formatting toolbar, and then click the Underline button.

Adding bold and underline

3. Click anywhere within the subject line to remove the highlighting. As you can see, these two simple changes have a dramatic effect on the document:

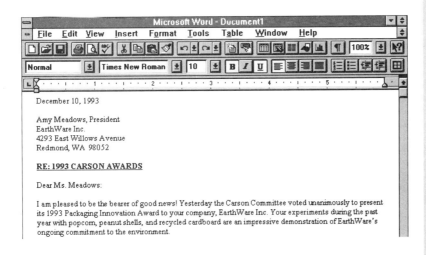

Moving toolbars

Convert any toolbar into a floating toolbar by double-clicking an empty spot between buttons. Move the floating toolbar anywhere on the screen by dragging its title bar. Double-clicking an empty spot on a floating toolbar repositions the toolbar at the top of the document window. You can also drag a toolbar to a new position on the screen. If you drag to the sides or bottom of the screen, the toolbar arranges itself along the edge of the document window. If you drag elsewhere, the toolbar becomes a floating toolbar.

Notice that the Bold and Underline buttons are now lighter and appear to be "pressed," indicating that those formats have been applied to the character to the left of the insertion point.

Now let's experiment with the document's font and font size:

1. Move the pointer into the selection bar, hold down Ctrl, and click the left mouse button to select the entire document.

Changing the font

2. Click the down arrow to the right of the Font box (the second downward-pointing arrow from the left on thc Formatting toolbar) to display a list of the fonts available with your printer. Use the scroll bar to the right of the list to bring the top of the list into view, and click Arial. The setting in the Font box changes to reflect the new font.

Changing the font size

3. Click the down arrow to the right of the Font Size box, and then click 12 in the drop-down list.

4. Now click a blank area of your screen so that you can see the results:

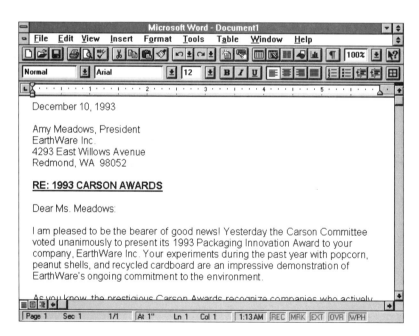

Font size

Fonts are measured in terms of their height—the distance from the bottom of *descenders* (the part of letters such as *p* that descend below the line) to the top of *ascenders* (the part of letters such as *h* that ascend above the line). The unit of measure is called a *point* (abbreviated *pt*), and 1 point equals 1/72 inch.

5. Try selecting other fonts and sizes from the Font and Font Size lists, and then return the entire document to the original font and size, Times New Roman and 10.

The Formatting toolbar always reflects the formats of the selected text. If no text is selected, the Formatting toolbar reflects the formats of the character to the left of the insertion point, except when the insertion point is at the beginning of a paragraph, in which case the Formatting toolbar reflects the formats of the character to the right. Watch the Formatting toolbar as you follow these steps:

Displaying the current format

1. Press Ctrl+Home to move the insertion point to the first character in the document. The Formatting toolbar indicates that the formatting of the character to the right of the insertion point is left-aligned.

2. Click an insertion point in the subject line. The settings on the Formatting toolbar change to reflect its formatting.

3. Select the entire document. Now none of the buttons on the Formatting toolbar are "pressed." If you select a chunk of text that is formatted in different ways, the Formatting toolbar can no longer reflect the current format.

We've changed the character formatting of parts of the letter. Now we'll try our hands at paragraph formatting. Let's take a look at the effects produced by the alignment buttons:

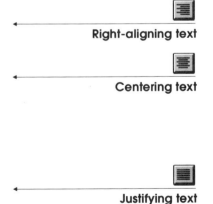

1. Press Ctrl+Home to move to the top of the letter, and click the Align Right button to right-align the date.

Right-aligning text

2. Next click an insertion point at the beginning of the subject line, and click the Center button.

Centering text

3. Click an insertion point anywhere in the letter's first main paragraph, hold down the Shift key, and press the Down Arrow key until at least one character in the second paragraph is selected. Then click the Justify button to tell Word to spread out the text so that the lines fill the space between the left and right margins.

Justifying text

4. Click anywhere in the text area to remove the highlighting so that you can see the results shown on the next page.

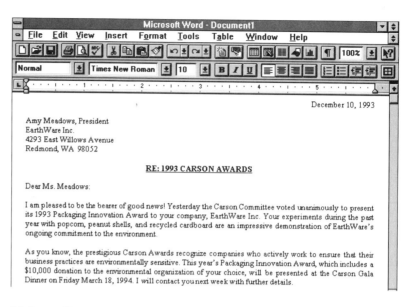

Using the Ruler

By default, Word 6 for Windows displays a horizontal ruler below the Formatting toolbar. This ruler can be used to set indents, tabs, column widths, and margins. We explore some of these features in later chapters. At the left end of the ruler is the Tab button, which you use to switch between four types of tabs: left, center, right, and decimal. The default is left. (See page 129 for more about tabs.)

Word also has a vertical ruler that appears when you view your documents in page layout view (see page 25).

Using the Menu Commands

Most of the buttons on the toolbars have equivalent commands on Word's menus. When a command is not represented by a toolbar button, or when you want to use a command with something other than its default settings, you can choose the command from a menu on the menu bar. In addition, you can choose some commands from shortcut menus, which appear when you click elements of your document or the window using the right mouse button. We look at both types of menus in this section.

Choosing Menu Bar Commands

Because the procedure for choosing menu bar commands is the same for all Windows applications, we assume that you

---

Paragraph marks

Paragraph marks not only indicate the ends of paragraphs, but they also store paragraph formatting. If you delete a paragraph mark, its paragraph becomes part of the following paragraph and assumes that paragraph's formatting. (If the deletion is a mistake, click the Undo button to restore the paragraph mark; see page 45.)

are familiar with it, and we provide only a quick review here. If you are a new Windows user, we suggest that you spend a little time becoming familiar with the mechanics of menus, commands, and dialog boxes before proceeding.

To choose a command from a menu on the menu bar, you first click the name of the menu. When the menu drops down, you simply click the name of the command you want. From the keyboard, you can press Alt to activate the menu bar, and then press the underlined letter of the name of the menu you want. To move from one open menu to another, use the Left and Right Arrow keys. When you have located the command you want, press its underlined letter, or press the Down Arrow key to highlight the desired command and then press Enter.

Choosing commands with the mouse

Choosing commands with the keyboard

Some command names are displayed in gray letters, indicating that you cannot choose those commands. For example, the Paste command on the Edit menu appears in gray until you use the Cut or Copy command, and the Cut and Copy commands appear in gray until you select some text.

Unavailable commands

Some command names are followed by an ellipsis (...), indicating that you must supply more information before Word can carry out the command. When you choose one of these commands, Word displays a dialog box. You can then supply the necessary information by typing in an edit box or by

Commands followed by ellipses

Dialog boxes

Custom menu bars

You can customize Word's menus with the commands, macros, fonts, styles, and AutoText entries that you use most often. Choose Customize from the Tools menu, and click the Menus tab in the Customize dialog box. In the Categories list, select the category of commands that you want to add (or select the All Commands category), and then select the command or other item you would like to add to a menu. Use the appropriate drop-down lists to specify the menu on which the command should appear and its position on the menu, and edit the supplied name as necessary. (The letter after the & sign is the shortcut key for the command.) In the Save Changes In drop-down list, specify the template you want the new menu attached to, click Add, and then click Close to close the Customize dialog box. To create a new custom menu, choose Customize from the Tools menu, and select the Menus tab. In the Save Changes In drop-down list, specify the template in which you want to save the new menu, and then click the Menu Bar button. Type the new menu's name in the Name On Menu Bar edit box, putting an & sign in front of the letter to be used as the menu's shortcut key, and use the Position On Menu Bar list to specify the location of the new menu. (Click First or Last and click the Add button, or highlight an existing menu and click the Add After button.) Click Close to return to the Customize dialog box, where you can add items to the menu as described earlier. To return the menus to their default settings, click Reset All in the Customize dialog box.

selecting options from lists, drop-down lists, or groups of check boxes and option buttons. Clicking a command button—usually OK—closes the dialog box and carries out the command according to your specifications. Clicking Cancel closes the dialog box and also cancels the command. Other buttons might be available to refine the original command or to open other dialog boxes with more options.

Let's run through the steps for choosing a command and do some useful exploring at the same time:

1. Click View on the menu bar. This menu provides commands for customizing the screen display. For example, the first four commands are mutually exclusive choices (the dot indicates mutual exclusivity) that determine how Word displays your documents. Because we talk about most of these commands elsewhere in the book, we won't discuss them here. For now, let's just play with the commands that affect screen layout.

Turning off the ruler

2. Choose the Ruler command from the View menu to turn off the ruler. (This command is a "toggle"; choosing it again will turn the command back on, as indicated by a check mark in front of the command name on the menu.)

Turning off the toolbars

3. Choose the Toolbars command from the View menu to display this dialog box:

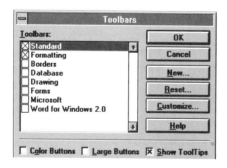

Microsoft toolbar

Selecting Microsoft from the Toolbars list in the Toolbars dialog box displays a floating toolbar with buttons you can click to start other Microsoft programs installed on your computer. Close the toolbar by double-clicking the Control menu at the left end of its title bar.

Here, you can select the toolbars you want to display by clicking their check boxes.

4. Click the Standard and Formatting check boxes to deselect them (remove the X), and then click OK. The top of your screen looks like this:

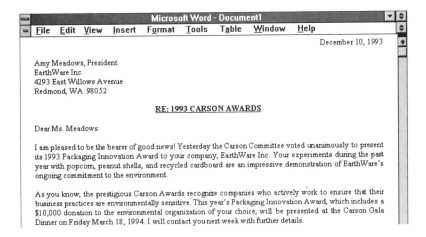

When you are working with a long document or have multiple documents displayed at one time, you might want to turn off these features so that you can see more of your text. (You can also hide the title bar, menu bar, toolbars, ruler, scroll bars, and status bar by choosing Full Screen from the View menu; click the Full Screen button to display them again.) When you quit Word, many of the settings that control the appearance of the screen are stored in the WINWORD.INI file in the directory containing Word for Windows. (This file is not to be confused with WIN.INI, which is stored in the WINDOWS directory.) The next time you start Word, the stored settings are used, so the screen looks as it did when you left it.

Preserving screen settings

5. Choose the Options command from the bottom of the Tools menu to display a dialog box something like this one:

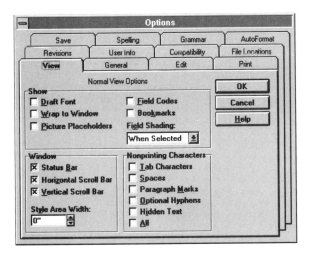

By selecting various options in this dialog box, you can control the display of many different screen elements. As you can see, the dialog box is multilayered, with each layer designated at the top of the dialog box by a tab like a file folder tab. The View options are currently displayed. (If they're not, click the View tab at the top of the dialog box.)

6. Deselect the Status Bar, Horizontal Scroll Bar, and Vertical Scroll Bar options in the Window section (there should be no Xs in their check boxes). Then select the All option in the Nonprinting Characters section. (You can also turn the display of specific nonprinting symbols on and off from this dialog box.) As you can see here, Word turns off the status bar and scroll bars, giving you a little more room for text, and turns on the display of nonprinting symbols.

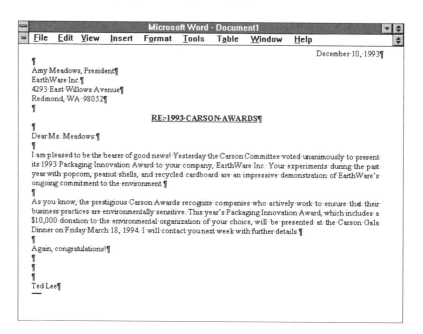

View options that increase efficiency

On the View tab of the Options dialog box, you can specify options that help speed up your work. Selecting the Draft Font and Picture Placeholders options can cut down the time Word takes to redraw the screen for documents with many fonts or graphics. Selecting Wrap To Window can speed up the editing of documents that are wider than the screen. (The text is wrapped for display purposes only; your margins remain the same.)

7. Choose the Ruler command from the View menu to toggle on the ruler. Next choose Toolbars, select the Standard and Formatting options, and click OK. Then choose Options from the Tools menu, turn the status bar and scroll bars back on, and click OK.

If the nonprinting symbols bother you, click the Show/Hide ¶ button on the Standard toolbar to turn them all off.

Choosing Shortcut Menu Commands

For efficiency, the commands that you are likely to use with a particular element of a document, such as ordinary text or a running head, are combined on special menus, called *shortcut menus*. Shortcut menus are also available for window elements, such as the toolbars. You access an element's shortcut menu by pointing to that element and clicking the right mouse button. This action is called *right-clicking*. Try the following:

Right-clicking

1. Point to one of the toolbars, and right-click to display the toolbar shortcut menu. You can select a specific toolbar directly from the menu that appears, or you can choose the Toolbars command to display the same dialog box that you see when you choose Toolbars from the View menu.

2. Click anywhere outside the menu to close it without choosing a command.

3. Point anywhere within the text of the letter, and right-click to display the shortcut menu for text. As you can see, this menu gives you instant access to editing and formatting commands.

4. Now press the Esc key to close the menu without choosing a command.

Using Keyboard Shortcuts

Although you can get by in Word using only the keyboard, frankly we don't know why you would want to. Using a mouse makes working with any Windows application much easier, and Word is no exception. However, if you prefer to use the keyboard, you can access many Word commands by using keyboard shortcuts. Here's an example:

Help with shortcuts

Word's list of keyboard shortcuts is extensive, and it would take a lot of space to reproduce it here. For more information about keyboard shortcuts, choose Index from the Help menu, and locate the Shortcuts entry. (See page 27 for more information about using the Help system.)

1. Select the words *1993 Packaging Innovation Award* in the first paragraph, and press Ctrl+I to italicize the text.

2. Select *Carson Gala Dinner on Friday March 18, 1994* in the second paragraph, and press Ctrl+I again.

You can achieve the same effect by clicking the Italic button on the toolbar. Similarly, pressing Ctrl+B and Ctrl+U are the keyboard equivalents of clicking the Bold and Underline buttons.

Saving Documents

Now would be a good time to save the letter so that it is available for future use. To save a new document, you click the Save button or choose Save As from the File menu. Word displays a dialog box in which you specify the name of the document. Thereafter, clicking the Save button or choosing the Save command saves the document without displaying the dialog box because the document already has a name. Let's save the document now on your screen:

Saving a new document

1. Choose Save As from the File menu. Word displays the Save As dialog box:

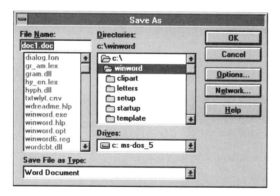

Word suggests DOC1.DOC as the name for the letter, but you should use a more descriptive name.

2. With DOC1.DOC highlighted, type *pi_award* (for *packaging innovation award*) in the File Name edit box. (You don't need to supply an extension; Word automatically uses DOC if you don't specify something else.)

3. Click OK. When you return to the document window, notice that the name PI_AWARD.DOC has replaced Document1 in the title bar.

From now on, you can click the Save button any time you want to save changes to this document. Because Word knows the name of the document, it simply saves the document by overwriting the previous version with the new version.

Filenames and extensions

Files are usually assigned a name and an extension separated by a period. Filenames cannot have more than eight characters, and extensions cannot have more than three. They can both consist of letters, numbers, and these characters:

_ ^ $! # % & - { } ( )

They can't contain spaces, commas, or periods.

Earlier versions of Word automatically created a backup file of a saved document. Instead of overwriting the previous version, Word assigned the BAK extension to it so that the previous version was available if you needed to return to it. Although Word no longer creates this file automatically, you can request that it retain a BAK file of each of your documents. Follow these steps:

1. Choose Options from the Tools menu, and click the Save tab in the Options dialog box to display these options:

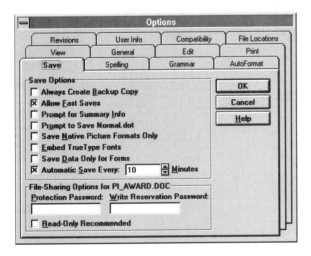

2. Select the Always Create Backup Copy option, and click OK.

3. Now click the Save button. Behind the scenes, Word renames the previous copy of the letter as PI_AWARD.BAK and assigns the name PI_AWARD.DOC to the current version.

If you want to save the changes you have made to a document but preserve the previous version, you can assign a different name to the new version by choosing the Save As command from the File menu, entering the new name in the File Name edit box, and clicking OK.

Opening Existing Documents

In this section, we show you how to open a document that you have already worked with. Follow the steps on the next page to open PI_AWARD.BAK.

Saving in a different directory

The file will be saved in the directory designated by the path above the Directories list. For example, the path C:\WINWORD means that the file will be saved in the WINWORD directory on your C drive. If you want to store the file in a different directory, you need to switch to the correct directory before you click OK to save the file. Double-click a directory icon in the Directories list to select that directory, display its files in the File Name list, and display its subdirectories in the Directories list. Double-click a subdirectory icon to display its files and subdirectories, and so on.

1. Click the Open button on the toolbar. Word displays a dialog box something like this one:

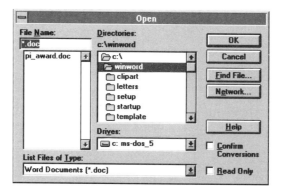

The File Name list shows the file with the DOC extension in the current directory. (The current directory's pathname is displayed below the word *Directories*.)

Using the * wildcard

2. You want to open PI_AWARD. BAK, so type *.*bak* in the File Name edit box, and press Enter to tell Word to display the names of all the files with the BAK extension.

3. Select PI_AWARD.BAK, and click OK. Word opens the specified document in its own window.

Creating New Documents

You now have two documents open on your screen, though PI_AWARD.DOC is totally obscured by PI_AWARD.BAK. For good measure, let's open a third document, this time a brand new one. Follow this step:

1. Click the New button on the toolbar.

That's all there is to it. A new document called Document3 is displayed on your screen, on top of PI_AWARD.BAK and PI_AWARD.DOC.

Manipulating Windows

Now that we have a few windows to play with, we'll pause here to review some window basics. Being able to work with more than one document open at a time is useful, especially if you need to use the same information in different docu-

Wildcards

The asterisk (*) is a *wildcard* that can be used to represent groups of characters or even entire names and extensions. (You can also use ? to represent a single character.) Representing file-names or extensions with * is a powerful technique because it allows you to designate groups of files. For example, *.DOC designates all files with the DOC extension, no matter what their name; AWARD.* designates all files with the name AWARD, no matter what their extension; and *.* designates all files, no matter what their name or extension.

ments. For example, you might use roughly the same text in a letter, a press release, a memo to employees, and a newsletter to clients. Follow these steps to see how easy it is to move from one document to another:

1. Click Window on the menu bar to display the commands on the Window menu. The three open documents are listed at the bottom of the menu, with a check mark beside Document3 to indicate that its window is active.

2. Choose PI_AWARD.DOC from the list of open documents. Word brings the letter to the top of the stack of windows.

3. Choose Arrange All from the Window menu. Word arranges the three open documents so that they each occupy about a third of the screen, like this:

Arranging windows

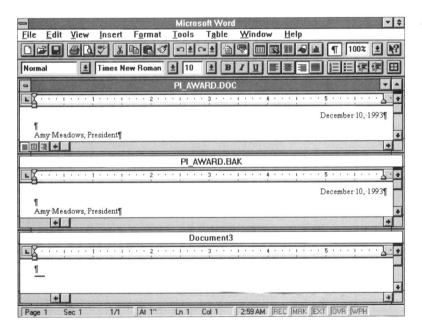

4. Click anywhere in PI_AWARD.BAK to activate it. Notice that the title bar of the active document is darker than the other two title bars. Any entries you make and most commands you choose will affect only the active document.

The active window

5. Click the PI_AWARD.BAK window's Maximize button. The window expands to fill the screen, completely obscuring the other two documents.

Maximizing a window

Opening a second view →
6. Choose the New Window command from the Window menu. Word opens a window that displays a second view of the active document, allowing you to see one part of the document while you edit another. The new window's title bar reads *PI_AWARD.BAK:2*.

7. Now open the Window menu. The original PI_AWARD.BAK file has become PI_AWARD.BAK:1 and is followed on the menu by PI_AWARD.BAK:2. Close the menu by clicking anywhere outside it.

Here's another way to see two parts of the same document at the same time:

Splitting a window →
1. Move the pointer to the thin black box, called the *split box*, just above the up scroll arrow in the vertical scroll bar. The pointer changes to a double horizontal bar with up and down arrows.

2. Drag the split box downward to the position at which you want to split the PI_AWARD.BAK window into panes. When you release the mouse button, your screen looks like this:

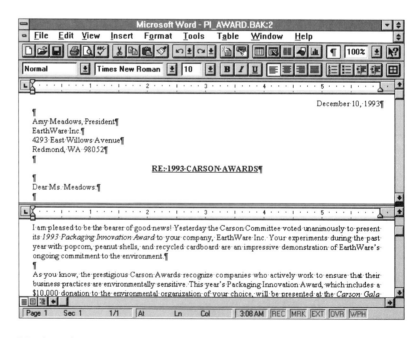

Notice that you now have two rulers and two vertical scroll bars, one set for each "pane."

3. In the bottom pane, click the vertical scroll bar below the scroll box. Notice that the text in the bottom pane scrolls, while the text in the top pane remains stationary.

Scrolling panes independently

4. To remove the pane, you can drag the split box back to its original location below the Formatting toolbar, or you can double-click the split box. But here's another way: Choose Remove Split from the Windows menu.

Removing a pane

These simple techniques work equally well no matter how many documents you have open. (We've found that three is the practical limit if you want to be able to see them all at the same time and do useful work.)

Closing Documents

When you've finished working with a document, it's wise to close it to conserve your computer's memory for the work at hand. We'll use one method to close PI_AWARD.BAK:2 and another to close PI_AWARD.BAK:1, and yet another to close Document3:

1. With PI_AWARD.BAK:2 still active, choose Close from the Document Control menu at the left end of the menu bar (see the figure on page 3). Word then closes the second view of the document. The title bar of PI_AWARD.BAK:1 reverts to plain old PI_AWARD.BAK to indicate that it is the only window displaying this document.

2. With PI_AWARD.BAK active, double-click the Document Control menu's icon at the left end of the menu bar (*not* the Application Control menu's icon at the end of the title bar). If you have made inadvertent changes to the document, Word asks whether you want to save the document. Click No to discard the changes and close the document.

3. Choose Document3 from the Window menu, and then choose Close from the File menu.

Now only the current version of the letter is still open on your screen.

Printing Documents

For all the talk in the popular press about a paperless office, the end product of a word-processing session is usually a printed document, whether you are writing a letter, a newsletter, or an annual report. Before you print from Word for the first time, you will need to check that your printer setup is correct. And before you print any document, you will want to check that all its elements are in place. Then printing is usually a simple matter of clicking the Print button on the toolbar. If you can print from any other Windows application, you should have no trouble printing from Word.

Setting Up for Printing

When you installed Windows, you indicated which printers you had available. These printers can all be accessed by Word, but only one at a time. You select a printer as follows:

Selecting a printer

1. Choose Print from the File menu to see this dialog box:

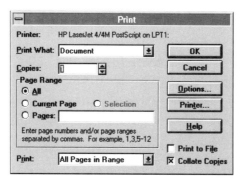

Here you can indicate the number of copies to print and the specific pages to be printed.

2. Click the Printer button to display a dialog box like this one:

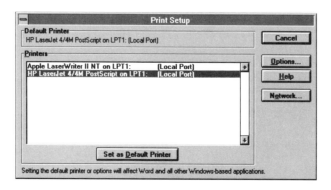

3. If more than one printer is listed in the Printers list, select the one you want to use, click Set As Default Printer, and then click Close twice return to your document.

Selecting a printer

Previewing Documents

The letter you have created is only one page long and it has no headers or footers (see the discussion on page 94). However, it is worth checking even a document this small in print preview to get an idea of how it will look on the page when it is printed. Follow these steps to preview the letter:

1. Click the Print Preview button on the toolbar. Word displays the entire page, like this:

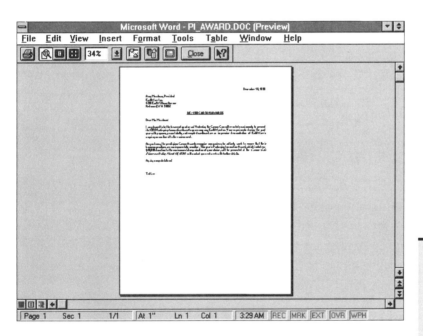

Editing is possible in print preview but not very practical. Word automatically removes the Standard and Formatting toolbars and displays the Print Preview toolbar.

2. Move the pointer over the buttons on this toolbar, pausing so that ToolTips can display each button's name and description. If your display is scaled to show more than one page, switch views by clicking the One Page button.

3. Click the View Ruler button to display both horizontal and vertical rulers. If you needed to, you could adjust the margins of the document using these rulers.

Page layout view

A third way of viewing your document, page layout view, also displays your document as it will appear on the printed page, with headers, footers, and graphics in place. You switch to page layout view by choosing Page Layout from the View menu or by clicking the Page Layout View button at the left end of the horizontal scroll bar. In this view, you can also display your document at various percentages of magnification, including whole page and two page views, by using the Zoom Control box on the toolbar.

4. Now click the Close button to return to Normal view.

Straightforward Printing

You can print directly from print preview by clicking the Print button on the Print Preview toolbar. Here's how you print your document from Normal view:

Quick printing

1. Click the Print button on the toolbar.

That's it! Word prints the active document with the settings currently specified in the Print dialog box shown on page 24. If you want to change the number of copies or the range of pages to be printed, you must choose Print from the File menu and make the necessary changes in the Print dialog box. For example, if you change the number of copies to 2 and click OK, Word prints two copies of the letter.

Changing the number of copies

Rather than explain the printing options in detail here, we'll move on to the next section, where we show you how to get information about these options and other Word features.

Getting Help

This has been a whistle-stop tour of Word, and you might not remember everything we've covered. If you forget how to carry out a particular task, help is never far away. You've already seen how the ToolTips feature can jog your memory about the functions of the toolbar buttons. Here we'll look at some other ways to get information.

Looking at the Status Bar

One often-overlooked source of help is the status bar. While you work on your document, the status bar displays such information as (from left to right) the page number, the section number, and how many pages are in the document; the insertion point's location; the current time; and the status of five Word features (for example, the EXT indicator is highlighted when you turn on Extend-Selection mode).

Print specifications

To print multiple copies of a document from the Print dialog box, enter the number of copies in the Copies edit box. If you don't want Word to collate the copies, click the Collate Copies check box to deselect it. To print only the page containing the insertion point, click the Current Page option. To print selected pages, click the Pages option, and then enter the page numbers (for example, *2–4* for pages 2, 3, and 4; and *2,4* for pages 2 and 4 only). In the Print What edit box, specify what you want to print. (You can print specific elements by selecting from the Print What drop-down list.) In the Print edit box, specify whether you want to print all, all odd, or all even pages. Finally, click Print To File to "print" an image of the document to a file on disk.

When you highlight a command on a menu, the status bar displays a description of the command. You can search through the menus, using the Arrow keys to move the highlight to each command and checking its description in the status bar. When you point to a toolbar button, the status bar displays its description (whether ToolTips is turned on or off).

Displaying command
descriptions

Displaying button descriptions

Using the Help System

You can access Word's Help system in several ways. First let's use Word's Help menu:

1. Choose Contents from the Help menu. Clicking any of the options in the Word Help Contents window takes you to topic lists that enable you to find the information you need.

2. Press the F1 key to get information about using Help, click Move Around In Help in the list of topics, and then click the Maximize button in the top-right corner of the window. Your screen now looks like this:

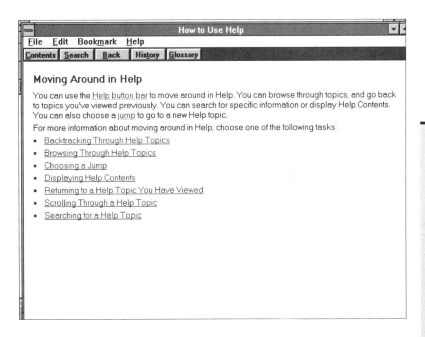

Examples and demos

You can choose Examples And Demos from the Help menu to display a list of features about which you can obtain graphic explanations. Clicking a feature displays an annotated example, and clicking the Demo button in the bottom-right corner of the Example screen opens a short animated demonstration of how to use that feature. You can click a button to see each step, or click Close to return to the graphic example and to the initial list of features.

3. Click topics with dotted underscores to display pop-up definitions and topics with solid underscores to jump to related information. When you are finished, click the Back button until you return to the Word Help Contents window.

4. Explore any other Help topics that interest you, and then choose the Exit command from Help's File menu to return to your document.

Another way to access Help is using the Help button on the toolbar. Try this:

Searching for a topic

1. Double-click the Help button to display the Search dialog box:

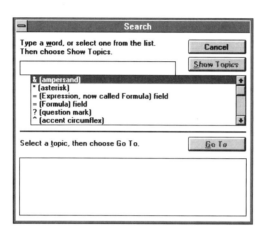

This dialog box can also be accessed by choosing Search For Help On from the Help menu or by clicking the Search button on the Help toolbar.

2. In turn, press the P, R, and I keys. Word scrolls the Search list to display topics beginning with *pri*.

3. Select *Print command (File menu)*, and then click the Show Topics button. Word displays a list of all the topics related to this subject. With *Print command (File menu)* selected, click the Go To button to jump directly to that Help topic.

4. Choose Exit from the File menu to leave Help.

You can also get immediate information about the task at hand—printing, for example:

1. Click the Help button on the toolbar once, move the question-mark pointer to File on the menu bar, and click to drop down the menu as usual. Then click Print. Word displays the same Help topic you saw earlier.

The Help index

You can use the Help index to find information about a specific topic. Simply choose Index from the Help menu, and click the letter at the top of the dialog box that corresponds to the first letter of the topic you're interested in. Then click the topic to display the information.

2. Double-click the Control-menu icon in the top-left corner of the Help window to return to your document.

The Help button can give you information about your document's formatting and about elements of the document window. Try this:

1. Click the Help button, move the question-mark pointer over the letter, and then click the mouse button to see information about the formatting of the text under the pointer, like this:

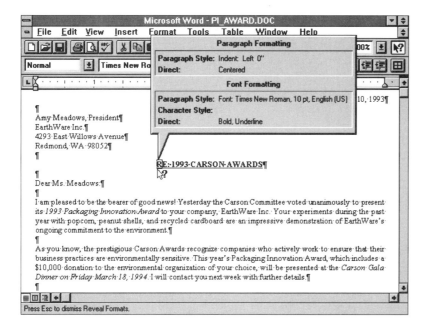

2. Press the Esc key to remove the information.

Quitting Word

Well, that's it for the basic tour. We'll finish up by showing you how to end a Word session:

1. Choose Exit from the File menu.

2. If Word asks whether you want to save the changes you have made to the letter, click Yes.

We'll work with the letter again in Chapter 3.

Help with dialog boxes

All dialog boxes include a Help button that you can click to move directly to the Help topic for the appropriate command. You can quickly review the section of the topic devoted to the dialog box options and then return to the dialog box by choosing Exit from Help's File menu.

Letter-Perfect Documents: Producing a Company Backgrounder

What you will learn...

Assign heading levels and reorganize your documents in outline view

Redmond Business Environmental Action Team

What is Redmond BEAT?

Redmond BEAT (Business Environmental Action Team) is a local chapter of USA BEAT, a network of companies who are actively working to ensure that their business operations are based on sound environmental practices.

Find and replace text to maintain consistency

How does it work?

Member companies agree to participate in two ongoing efforts: 1. They pledge to scrutinize their operations and wherever possible, implement procedures that will minimize any adverse effects on the environment. 2. They agree to field-test new "environmentally kind" products and services to evaluate their potential impact on both company costs and the environment.

When was it started?

Redmond BEAT was founded in 1989. USA BEAT, which currently has 210 local chapters, was founded in 1987.

Use AutoText and AutoCorrect for often-used text

Why was it started?

The chartering of Redmond BEAT was spearheaded by long-time Redmond resident William Henry, President of Creative GlassWorks. Struck by the incongruity between his family's efforts to recycle household waste and the fact that his company was sending several dumpsters of garbage to the Redmond landfill every month, Henry began looking for other ways to dispose of the packaging in which his company received raw materials. His questions caused one of his suppliers, Jordan Manufacturing, to explore alternative packaging methods. The result was less garbage in the Creative GlassWorks dumpsters at no additional cost and negligible other effects for either company. In the meantime, Henry learned about USA BEAT, and a few months of persuasive campaigning later, Redmond BEAT became the newest chapter of a rapidly growing national association.

Who can join?

Membership in Redmond BEAT is open to all companies licensed to do business in the city of Redmond.

Why should my company join?

Current members cite two main reasons for joining. Many companies are managed by people who were attracted to this area by its natural beauty and who want to be a part of the effort to preserve it. Other companies stress the potential advantages in today's competitive markets of being perceived as a "green" company by consumers who are increasingly environmentally aware.

How can I find out more?

Come to a meeting. Redmond BEAT meets at 8:00 AM on the last Tuesday of every month in the Community Center. For more information, contact Ted Lee at 555-6789.

Check spelling and grammar to avoid embarrassments

Delete, copy, and move text until it reads exactly right

With Word for Windows, you can apply fancy formats and add graphics and special effects to increase the impact of a document. But all the frills in the world won't compensate for poor organization and spelling or grammatical errors. That's why this chapter focuses on the Word tools that help you develop and refine the content of your documents. First we look at Word's AutoText and AutoCorrect features, which help ensure the accuracy of what you type. Then we cover basic editing skills, as well as searching and replacing. Finally, we discuss checking your spelling and grammar. By the end of this chapter, you'll know how to ensure that your writing is correct and your organization is solid, and you'll be ready to learn how to make your documents look good.

Backgrounders

As our example for this chapter, we create a "backgrounder" for an association called Redmond Business Environmental Action Team (BEAT). Backgrounders provide general information about a company or organization, and they are often mailed out with press releases and other promotional materials. First let's enter a few headings to establish the basic structure of the document:

1. Start with a new document on your screen. If you have an existing document open, use one of the techniques we showed you in Chapter 1 to close it (see page 23), and then click the New button on the toolbar to open a new blank document.

2. If the ruler is displayed on your screen, turn it off by choosing the Ruler command from the View menu. That way, you'll have a bit more room to work.

3. Type *What is Redmond BEAT?* and press Enter. Word enters the heading, inserts a paragraph mark, and moves the insertion point to the next line. (If you don't see the paragraph mark, click the Show/Hide ¶ button on the toolbar; see page 8 for more information.)

4. Type *Why was it started?* and press Enter.

5. Continue entering the headings shown here (we've magnified the document to make it easier to read):

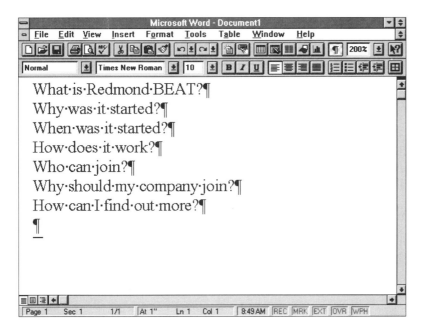

6. Now save the document by clicking the Save button, specifying *bkground.doc* as the name of the file, and clicking OK.

We're going to use the backgrounder in other chapters in this book, so let's create a document summary to make the backgrounder easier to find. Filling in summary information might seem time-consuming and irrelevant now, when you have only a couple of files to deal with. However, after you accumulate many files in several directories, you could find yourself relying on this information to quickly locate the file you need. So you might want to get in the habit now of creating document summaries, using as many of the edit boxes as you can and being as precise as possible about the contents of each file.

Document summaries

1. Choose Summary Info from the File menu to display a dialog box similar to this one:

Keywords

To use keywords effectively, you need to come up with a list of topics that can be applied to most of your documents. For example, Ted Lee might have a list of keywords such as Awards, Projects, Membership, Fund-raising, Special Events, and so on. By entering the appropriate keywords in the Summary Info dialog box, he can then easily locate all documents pertaining to a specific topic. If you assign keywords "on the fly" as you create each document, you may find it difficult to remember them all, and your keywords will be less useful for locating categories of documents.

As you can see, Word has already entered information such as the name of the file and which directory it's stored in. The program has also taken a guess at the document's title, based on the first line of the backgrounder.

2. Type *Backgrounder*, and press Tab. Your entry replaces the selected title, and the insertion point moves to the next edit box, ready for you to enter the document's subject.

3. Type *Redmond BEAT*, and press Tab again.

4. Word has filled in the Author edit box with the name that was entered when the program was installed on your computer. If the Author edit box displays your name, press Tab to move on. If it doesn't, type your name, and then press Tab.

This information should be enough to enable us to identify the file later, so we won't fill in the remaining edit boxes for this document. But let's take a moment to look at some of the other information Word stores for each document:

Displaying document statistics → 1. Click the Statistics button to display this dialog box:

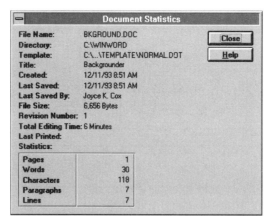

As you can see, Word keeps track of when the document was created and revised; how long you have worked on this document; and the number of pages, words, characters, paragraphs, and lines.

2. Click Close and then OK to close the dialog boxes and attach the summary information to the file.

Now let's add some text under a couple of the headings:

Quick counting

To obtain a quick count of the number of pages, words, characters, paragraphs, and lines in a document, choose Word Count from the Tools menu. Word displays a dialog box with all the counts listed. You can have Word include footnotes and endnotes in the count by selecting the Include Footnotes And Endnotes option. Click Close to close the dialog box.

1. Click an insertion point between the question mark and the paragraph mark at the end of the *What is Redmond BEAT?* heading, press Enter, and type the following:

   Redmond BEAT (Business Environmental Action Team) is a local chapter of National BEAT, a network of companies who are actively working to ensure that their business operations are based on sound environmental practices.

2. Click an insertion point between the question mark and the paragraph mark at the end of the *Why was it started?* heading, press Enter, and type the following:

   The chartering of Redmond

   There's *Redmond* again; that's the third time you've had to type it. Let's look at a couple of ways you can save keystrokes and ensure that the words and phrases you use repeatedly are always entered correctly.

Storing and Retrieving Often-Used Text

To help you enter often-used text efficiently, accurately, and consistently, Word has two special features: AutoText and AutoCorrect. At first glance these two features seem almost identical; they both enable you to store text or a graphic with a name and then insert the text or graphic in any document at any time simply by typing the name. An AutoText or Auto-correct entry can be as short as a single text character or as long as several pages of text or graphics, and it can include formatting. Unlike the contents of the Clipboard, AutoText and AutoCorrect entries are saved from one Word session to the next. So what's the difference between them? To insert an AutoText entry, you type the entry's name and then press the F3 key. To insert an AutoCorrect entry, you simply type the name; the instant you press the Spacebar to move on to the next word or type a punctuation mark, Word automatically replaces the name with its entry.

How do you decide which to use? Here's an example. Suppose you own a landscaping business. You know you'd save a lot of time and effort if you could type *aspen* instead of having to type and italicize *Populus tremuloides* (the botanical name for the aspen tree) every time you include this tree

AutoText and AutoCorrect

Saving AutoText entries

Word saves AutoText entries with a particular template. You can specify whether an AutoText entry is to be saved with the Normal template, in which case the entry will be available for use in all documents you create, or with the template attached to the current document (if it is not the Normal template). You specify the storage location in the Make AutoText Entry Available To drop-down list in the AutoText dialog box.

in a materials list for your wholesaler. But when you communicate with your clients, you want to be able to refer to the aspen tree by its common name rather than its botanical name. This entry is a prime candidate for AutoText because you can control when Word replaces the name *aspen* with the entry *Populus tremuloides* and when it stays plain old *aspen*. If you use AutoCorrect instead, Word will always replace the name *aspen* with *Populus tremuloides*. Let's try both features.

Using AutoText

As we said, you use Word's AutoText feature to store text and graphics that you want to be able to retrieve manually. For this example, we'll turn a word we have already typed into an AutoText entry. Follow along as we simplify the typing of *Redmond*:

1. Select the word *Redmond* that you just typed, and choose AutoText from the Edit menu to display this dialog box:

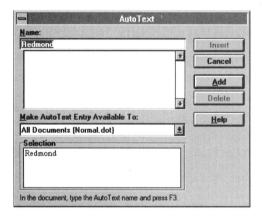

Word displays the selected text in both the Name edit box and the Selection box at the bottom of the dialog box.

2. Type *red* in the Name edit box, and click the Add button. Word closes the dialog box.

Now let's use the entry we've just created as we write a few more paragraphs for the backgrounder:

1. Click an insertion point after *Redmond* in the paragraph that begins *The chartering of Redmond*, type a space, and then type the following (don't press the Spacebar after *red*):

BEAT was spearheaded by long-time red

2. Press F3. Word replaces *red* with the *Redmond* entry.

3. Continue typing the following paragraph, using the *red-F3* sequence to insert *Redmond* where indicated. Be sure to type the error marked in bold exactly as you see it so that you will have a mistake to correct later in the chapter. Also include the **** characters, which are placeholders for information we'll add later.

resident William Henry, President of Creative GlassWorks. Struck by the incongruity between his family's efforts to recycle household waste and the fact that his company was sending several dumpsters of garbage to the red-F3 *landfill every month, Henry began looking for other ways to dispose of the packaging in which his company received raw materials. His questions caused one of his suppliers, ****, to explore alternative packaging methods. The result was less garbage in the Creative GlassWorks dumpsters at no additional cost and negligible other effects for either company. In the meantime, Henry learned about National BEAT, and a few months of persuasive* **campaining** *later,* red-F3 *BEAT became the newest chapter of a rapidly growing national association.*

Suppose you forget the code for an AutoText entry. Does that mean you can't use the entry anymore? Not at all. Try this:

1. Click an insertion point at the end of the *How can I find out more?* heading, press Enter, and type *Come to a meeting* followed by a period and a space.

2. Choose AutoText from the Edit menu to see this dialog box:

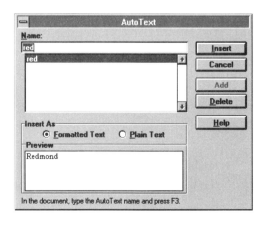

Deleting AutoText and AutoCorrect entries

To delete an AutoText entry, choose AutoText from the Edit menu, select the name of the entry you want to delete from the Name list, click the Delete button, and then click Close. To delete an AutoCorrect entry, choose Auto-Correct from the Tools menu, select the name of the entry you want to delete from the list at the bottom of the AutoCorrect dialog box, click the Delete button, and then click OK.

Previewing entries in the
AutoText dialog box

The name in the list box serves as a reminder of the entry you have created. If you create more than one entry, you can select them in turn and check the Preview box to see what each one represents.

3. With *red* selected in the list, click the Insert button. Word closes the dialog box and inserts the entry *Redmond* at the insertion point.

4. Finish typing the paragraph as follows:

   BEAT meets at 8:00 AM on the last Tuesday of every month in the Community Center.

   Now that we've simplified the typing of the word *Redmond*, you've probably noticed some other words that could benefit from the same treatment. How about *National BEAT* and *Redmond BEAT*? To simplify the typing of these entries, we'll use AutoCorrect.

Using AutoCorrect

Because Word automatically replaces AutoCorrect names with their entries, you should assign unique sequences of characters that you are not likely to use normally in a document as the names of AutoCorrect entries. Try this:

1. Select *Redmond BEAT* in the backgrounder's first heading but not the following space. Then choose AutoCorrect from the Tools menu to display this dialog box:

Bypassing AutoCorrect

To turn off AutoCorrect, deselect the Replace Text As You Type option in the AutoCorrect dialog box. If you don't want to turn off AutoCorrect but you also don't want AutoCorrect to replace a particular instance of a name with its entry, type the name, and after AutoCorrect replaces it, click the Undo button (see page 45).

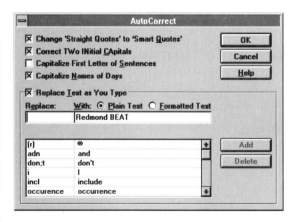

As you can see, Word is waiting for you to enter the name that you want replaced with the selected text, which appears in the With edit box. At the bottom of the AutoCorrect dialog box is a ready-made list of "words" to be replaced each time you type them.

2. In the Replace edit box, type *rb* as the name of the entry, and click Add. Word adds the name and its replacement to the list.

Assigning a name to an AutoCorrect entry

3. Type *nb* in the Replace edit box, double-click *Redmond* in the With edit box to select it, and type *National* and a space. The entry in the With edit box is now *National BEAT*. Click OK to close the dialog box.

Now let's use these AutoCorrect entries so that you can get a feel for what time-savers they can be:

1. Click an insertion point at the end of the *When was it started?* heading, press Enter, and type this:

   nb, *which currently has **** local chapters, was founded in 1987.* rb *was founded in 1990.*

2. Next, click an insertion point at the end of the *Who can join?* heading, press Enter, and type the following (be sure to misspell *the* as *teh*):

   Membership in rb *is open to all companies licensed to do business in* teh *city of* red-F3. *For more information, contact Ted Lee at 555-6789.*

Modifying AutoCorrect Entries

Modifying an AutoCorrect entry is as easy as creating one from scratch. Suppose you want to change the *National BEAT* entry to *USA BEAT*, but because you are in the habit of using the name *nb* to refer to the national association, you don't want to change the name. Follow these steps:

1. First select the word *National* in the paragraph under the *When was it started?* heading, and type *USA* in its place.

2. Now select *USA BEAT*, and choose AutoCorrect from the Tools menu.

3. In the AutoCorrect dialog box, type *nb*, the name for the entry you want to replace, and then click the Replace button.

AutoCorrect options

In the AutoCorrect dialog box are several options that take care of common typing "errors." By default, Word changes straight quotation marks (") to open (") and close (") quotation marks. It also corrects faulty capitalization—two initial capital letters in a word and sentences that don't begin with a capital letter—and capitalizes the days of the week. You can turn off any of these options by clicking the corresponding check box.

Word asks you to confirm that you want to replace the old AutoCorrect entry with the new selection.

4. Click Yes, and then click OK to close the AutoCorrect dialog box. From now on, typing *nb* will insert *USA BEAT* instead of *National BEAT*.

5. Safeguard your work by saving the document.

The backgrounder contains two other references to *National BEAT* that need updating. We'll leave these for now so that we can use them later as examples of how you can quickly substitute one bit of text for another.

Editing Basics

Most word-processing documents, whether a note to yourself or an annual report, are created with one or more rounds of typing and editing. Although you may not realize it, you have already done some simple editing in this chapter. If you've typed words incorrectly, you have probably deleted them by pressing the Backspace key and then typed them correctly. A couple of times you have selected a word in a dialog box and replaced it by typing a new one. In this section, we briefly cover some more ways of revising documents. We'll make a few changes to the backgrounder to get a feel for what's involved.

Deleting and Replacing Text

First let's quickly see how to make small changes by deleting, or "clearing," and replacing text. We'll start by adding a new paragraph to the backgrounder:

1. Click an insertion point at the end of the *Why should my company join?* heading, press Enter, and type the following (including the errors in bold and the AutoCorrect names, which are not italicized):

*Current members **site** two principal reasons for joining. Many companies are managed by people who were first attracted to this area by **it's** natural beauty* adn *who therefore want to be part of* teh *effort to preserve it. Other companies stress* teh *potential advantages in today's **competative** mar-*

*kets of being perceived as a "green" company by consumers who are increasingly **environmently** aware.*

2. Now for our first correction. Click an insertion point after the *a* in *competative*, press the Backspace key to delete the character to the left of the insertion point, and type *i*.

Deleting a character to the left

3. Next click an insertion point after the last *e* in *therefore*, and press Ctrl+Backspace to delete the word to the left of the insertion point.

Deleting a word to the left

4. Click an insertion point to the left of the *s* in *site*, press the Delete key to delete the character to the right of the insertion point, and type *c*.

Deleting a character to the right

5. Then click an insertion point to the left of the *f* in *first*, and press Ctrl+Delete to delete the word to the right of the insertion point. (You can also select the word *first* and choose Clear from the Edit menu.)

Deleting a word to the right

6. Finally, double-click the word *principal* in the first sentence, and type *main* as its replacement.

As you have seen, Word is by default in Insert mode, meaning that when you click an insertion point and begin typing, the characters you enter are inserted to the left of the insertion point, pushing any existing text to the right. Word can also operate in Overtype mode, meaning that when you click an insertion point and begin typing, each character you enter replaces an existing character.

Insert mode

Overtype mode

Let's experiment a bit with overtyping. Suppose Redmond BEAT was actually founded in 1989, not 1990. Here's how to make this simple correction:

1. Click an insertion point between the first and second 9s of 1990 under the *When was it started?* heading.

2. Press the Insert key. The letters *OVR* are highlighted in the status bar to indicate that you are now in Overtype mode.

3. Type *8*, which overtypes the second 9, and then type *9*, which overtypes the 0, so that the entry now correctly reads *1989*.

No automatic replacement

You can have Word insert what you type to the left of a selection instead of replacing it. Choose Options from the Tools menu, click the Edit tab to display the editing options, click the Typing Replaces Selection option to deselect it, and then click OK.

4. Press the Insert key to turn off Overtype mode. This step is important; you might overtype valuable information if you forget it.

Copying Text

You can copy any amount of text within the same document or to a different document. Copy operations can either be carried out using the Copy and Paste buttons or by using a mouse technique called *drag-and-drop editing*. Generally, you use drag-and-drop editing when copying text short distances; that is, when the text you're copying and the place you're copying it to can be viewed simultaneously. Try this:

Drag-and-drop editing

1. Use the vertical scroll bar to position the backgrounder on the screen so that both the *Who can join?* and *How can I find out more?* sections are visible at the same time.

2. Click an insertion point anywhere in the sentence that begins *For more information* under the *Who can join?* heading.

3. Press F8 three times—first to turn on Extend-Selection mode, second to highlight the word containing the insertion point, and third to highlight the sentence containing the selected word. Then press Esc to turn off Extend-Selection mode with the sentence still selected.

Copying text with
drag-and-drop editing

4. Point to the selected text, hold down the left mouse button, and drag the shadow insertion point to the right of the last period in the document (after *Community Center*). While still

Redefining the Insert key

If it annoys you that the Insert key activates Overtype mode instead of inserting the Clipboard contents at the insertion point, choose Options from the Tools menu, click the Edit tab to display the editing options, click the Use The INS Key For Paste option, and then click OK.

Smart editing

When you cut or copy and paste text, Word intuits where spaces are needed for the text to make sense. For example, it removes spaces before and adds spaces after punctuation marks. You can tell Word to leave these kinds of adjustments to you by choosing Options from the Tools menu, clicking the Edit tab, clicking the Use Smart Cut And Paste option to deselect it, and clicking OK.

Drag-and-drop problems

If pointing to a text selection and then holding down the mouse button creates an insertion point and deselects the text, the Drag-And-Drop Text Editing option is turned off. To turn it on, choose Options from the Tools menu, click the Edit tab, click Drag-And-Drop Text Editing, and then click OK.

holding down the mouse button, hold down the Ctrl key (a small plus sign appears next to the mouse pointer), and then release the key and the mouse button together. Immediately, a copy of the selected sentence appears in the location designated by the shadow insertion point, like this:

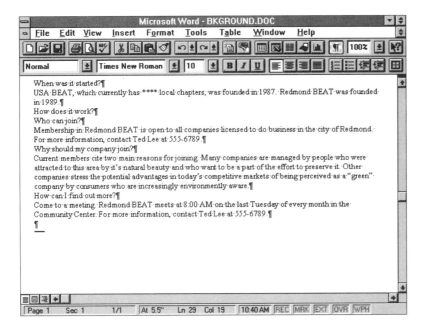

Now let's put the Copy and Paste buttons through their paces. This time we'll copy some text to a different document:

1. Select the entire paragraph under the *How can I find out more?* heading, and click the Copy button on the toolbar. Word stores a copy of the selected text in a temporary storage place in memory called the Clipboard.

Copying text with the toolbar

2. Click the New button on the toolbar to open a blank document, and then click the Paste button. Word inserts the copied sentence, and the new document now looks like this:

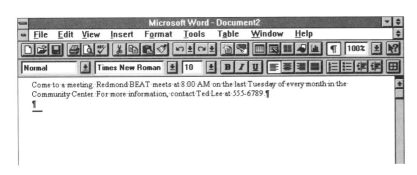

The original selection is still stored on the Clipboard, so if you needed to, you could paste another copy of the text without having to copy it again.

3. Choose Close from the File menu, and when Word asks if you want to save your changes, click No to close the Document2 window.

Moving Text

The procedure for moving text is similar to that for copying text. Try moving some text with the drag-and-drop technique:

1. With BKGROUND.DOC active, select the sentence that begins *USA BEAT* under the *When was it started?* heading, including the space after the period.

Moving text with drag-and-drop editing

2. Point to the highlighted text, hold down the left mouse button, drag the shadow insertion point after the period following 1989, and release the mouse button. The selected text moves to the specified location. You have, in effect, transposed the two sentences in this paragraph.

Now try using the cut-and-paste technique:

1. Select the *When was it started?* heading and the next paragraph.

Moving text with the toolbar

2. Click the Cut button on the toolbar. Word removes the text from the document and stores it on the Clipboard.

Let's pause here for a moment. The Clipboard can hold only one selection at a time, and clicking either Copy or Cut replaces the Clipboard's contents with the new selection. Suppose that in the middle of this move operation, you realize that the sentence that begins *For more information* is now repeated in two sections of the backgrounder. You want to delete the occurrence after the *Who can join?* heading without disturbing the contents of the Clipboard. You could position the insertion point after the period following the telephone number and press Backspace, but here's an easier way:

The Cut, Copy, and Paste commands

As alternatives to using the Cut, Copy, and Paste buttons, you can use the equivalent commands on either the Edit menu or the text shortcut menu (the menu that appears when you right-click selected text). The result of all three methods is identical.

3. With the insertion point in the first *For more information* sentence, press F8 three times to select the sentence, and then press Esc to turn off Extend-Selection mode.

4. Press the Delete key. Word removes the sentence without storing it on the Clipboard.

5. Now click an insertion point at the beginning of the *Why was it started?* heading (you may have to scroll upward), and click the Paste button to insert the cut text, like this:

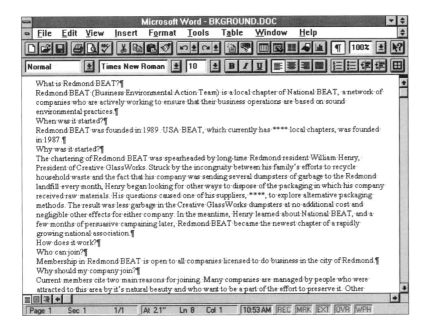

Undoing Commands

For those occasions when you make an editing mistake, Word provides a safety net: the Undo button. As you'll see if you follow these steps, Word can reverse many of your editing actions:

1. Click an insertion point in the paragraph under the *Who can join?* heading, and press F8 four times to select the paragraph (including the paragraph mark). Then press Delete. The paragraph is gone. Do you need to panic? No.

2. Now click the Undo button. Word reverses your previous editing action.

Undoing an edit

3. Click the down arrow to the right of the Undo button. Word displays a list of your previous editing actions.

4. Press Enter to restore the *For more information* sentence that you deleted (cleared) earlier.

Redoing an edit

5. You really don't need that sentence, so let's redo that last edit. Click the Redo button to redo your previous "undo."

Organizing Documents

The Outlining feature

You have seen how to move text around in a document using drag-and-drop editing and cut-and-paste techniques, but when a document has headings as well as ordinary text, it's often simpler to use Word's Outlining feature to move things around. Organizing a document is often a trial-and-error process. You start with the major topics, add a few subtopics, and then start tinkering with the organization, moving some headings and changing the level of others until you are satisfied. We realize that we will never convince some of you to use outlining, but after working with the examples in this section, others of you might decide, as we have, that outlining is a great tool for quickly rearranging paragraphs into their most logical order.

Most people are accustomed to thinking of outlining as the process that precedes the writing of lengthy documents. With Word, however, outlining is not a separate process but simply another way of looking at your document. Once you use Word's Outlining feature with a particular document, you can switch to outline view at any time to get an overview of your work. In this section, we'll set up the outline for the backgrounder and then use it to manipulate the document in various ways. Let's get started:

1. Choose Outline from the View menu. Word displays the Outline toolbar, which allows you to organize your document by assigning levels to the information on the screen. Because Word considers all the headings and paragraphs of the backgrounder to be ordinary body text, each one is identified in the selection area to its left by a small hollow square.

2. Move the pointer over the Outline toolbar, using ToolTips to get an idea of what each button does, and then press Ctrl+End to move to the end of the document.

Promoting body text

3. Type *Redmond Business Environmental Action Team*, and then click the Promote button on the Outline toolbar. Here's the result:

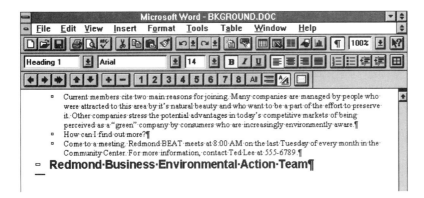

Word moves the heading to the left and reformats it to reflect its new status. Notice that Heading 1, the style that Word has applied to the heading, appears in the Style box at the left end of the Formatting toolbar. (See page 101 for more information about styles.) With Word, you can create up to nine heading levels, called Heading 1 through Heading 9. Also notice the large minus icon next to the heading; it indicates that the heading has no subheadings or text.

Heading styles

4. Click an insertion point anywhere in the *How can I find out more?* heading, and then click the Promote button. Repeat this step for each of the other headings.

5. Click the Show Heading 1 button. Word collapses the outline so that only the level 1 headings are visible:

Displaying a specific level

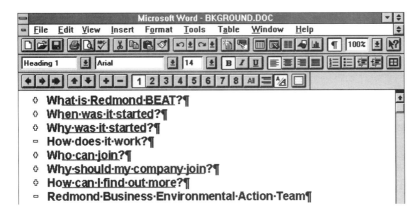

As already mentioned, a minus icon indicates that the heading doesn't have subordinate headings or text; a plus icon indicates that it does. In addition, Word puts a gray underscore beneath headings whose subordinate information is hidden.

Outline symbols

Now let's do a little reorganizing:

Moving a level up

1. Click an insertion point in the *Redmond Business Environmental Action Team* heading, and click the Move Up button on the Outline toolbar repeatedly until the heading is at the top of the document.

Moving a level down

2. Select both the *When was it started?* and *Why was it started?* headings, and then click the Move Down button once to move both headings below the *How does it work?* heading.

Expanding the outline

3. Click the Expand button on the Outline toolbar to display the body text below the two selected headings. As you can see, the paragraphs moved with their headings:

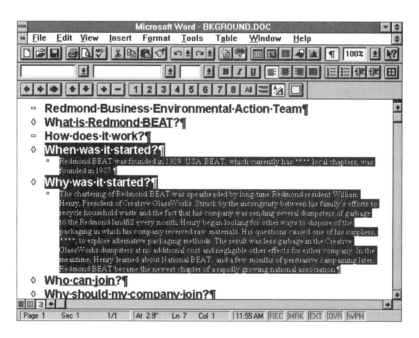

Collapsing the outline

4. Click the Collapse button to hide the text again.

What happens if you want to add information to the document while you are in outline view? Simple!

1. Click an insertion point at the end of the *How does it work?* heading, and press Enter. Word assumes you want to type another level 1 heading.

Converting to body text

2. Click the Demote To Body Text button on the Outline toolbar, and type the following, including the errors in bold:

*Member companies agree to participate in two ongoing efforts: 1. They pledge to scrutinize **there** operations and wherever possible, implement procedures that will minimize any adverse **affects** on the environment. 2. They agree to field-test new "**environmently** kind" products and services to evaluate their potential impact on both company costs and the environment.*

3. Click the Show 1 button to display only the headings.

Looking through the outline, you realize that all the headings except the first should really be level 2. You have seen how to use the Promote button to bump headings up one level. Here's how to bump them down:

1. Select all the headings except the first, and click the Demote button on the Outline toolbar. Word both moves the selected headings to the right so that their relationship to the level 1 heading above is readily apparent, and changes their formatting. In the Style box on the Formatting toolbar, Heading 2 is displayed. The minus icon to the left of the first heading changes to a plus icon, indicating that it now has subordinate headings and text.

Demoting headings

2. Click the Show All button to see these results:

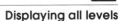

Displaying all levels

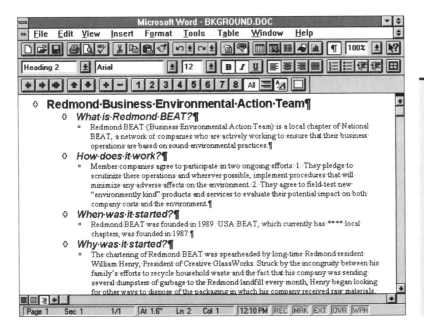

Deleting headings

To delete a heading from an outline, select the heading, and press Delete. If you want to also delete the heading's subordinate headings and text, collapse the outline before you make your selection. Otherwise, expand the outline before you select the heading so that you can see exactly which paragraphs will be affected when you press Delete.

Well, after that brief introduction to Word's Outlining feature, we'll return to normal view so that we can move on with the rest of the chapter:

Returning to normal view

1. Click the Normal View button at the left end of the horizontal scroll bar. Word removes the Outline toolbar, the plus icons, and the indenting but retains the formatting of the headings. In the selection area to the left of each heading is a square bullet indicating that the formatting is controlled by a style. (We talk more about styles on page 101.) Having set up the document's outline, you can return to outline view at any time by simply clicking the Outline View button at the left end of the horizontal scroll bar.

2. Click the Save button to save your work.

That quick tour of basic Word editing techniques should allow you to correct most mistakes and reorganize your documents with ease. But before we leave the topic of editing, we need to cover two related features that allow you to make broad-based changes efficiently.

Finding and Replacing

With Word, you can search a document for specific characters, formats, and styles. You can also specify replacement characters, formats, or styles. Because we don't cover formats and styles in this chapter, we focus here on finding and replacing text. You'll find a tip about finding and replacing formats on this page, and one about finding and replacing styles on page 109.

Finding Text

Finding a series of characters is easy. Being able to refine the search so that you locate precisely the characters you want takes a little practice. But once you know how to use the options Word provides, you will have no trouble zeroing in on any series of characters.

Recall that while typing the Redmond BEAT backgrounder, you left the characters **** as placeholders for information that needed to be added later. Suppose you now need to locate the placeholders so that you can substitute the correct information. In a document as short as the backgrounder, you

Finding and replacing formats

To search for text to which you have assigned a particular format, choose Find from the Edit menu, click the Format button, and then click Font for character formats or Paragraph for paragraph formats. In the Find Font or Find Paragraph dialog box, specify the format you want to find, click OK to return to the Find dialog box, and click Find Next. Word highlights the next text formatted with that format. You can use the Replace command to change a particular format. For example, to change all bold text to bold italic, choose Replace from the Edit menu, click Format and then Font, click Bold in the Font Style list, and click OK. Then click the Replace With edit box, click Format and then Font, click Bold Italic in the Font Style list, and click OK. Back in the Replace dialog box, click either Find Next and Replace or Replace All, depending on whether you want to confirm the replacement of each case of the specified format.

would have no difficulty locating ****. But if the current document were many pages long and several placeholders were involved, you would probably want to use the Find command to locate them. Here's how:

1. Press Ctrl+Home to move the insertion point to the top of the document.

2. Choose Find from the Edit menu. Word displays the dialog box shown here:

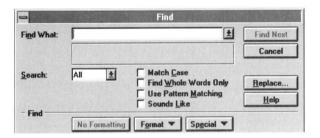

3. Enter **** in the Find What edit box.

4. Leave the other options as they are, and click Find Next. Word searches the document, stopping when it locates the first occurrence of ****.

5. Click Cancel to close the dialog box, and then type *210* to replace the highlighted placeholder.

6. Press Shift+F4 to repeat the Find command with the same Find What text and options as the previous search. Word locates the second ****.

Repeating a search

7. Replace the selection with *Jordan Manufacturing*.

If you are searching a large document and you want to be sure that you have substituted the correct information for all the placeholders, you can press Shift+F4 to search again. Word searches to the end of the document and then asks whether to continue from the beginning of the document. Click Yes to have Word search the document again. If you are searching from the Find dialog box and Word does not find any occurrences of the Find What text, it displays another dialog box to let you know that it couldn't find the text. Click No to end

Editing during a search or replace

You can edit your document in the middle of a search or replace operation without closing the Find or Replace dialog box. Simply click the document window to activate it, make your changes, and then click anywhere in the Find or Replace dialog box to continue your search or replace.

the search. If you are searching with Shift+F4, Word doesn't display this dialog box.

Most of your searches will be as simple as this one was, but you can also refine your searches by using the options in the Find dialog box and by entering special characters, as follows:

Search options

- Use the drop-down list of Search options to search forward to the end of the document (Down) or backward to the beginning of the document (Up) from the insertion point, or to search the entire document (All).

Match Case option

- Click the Match Case option to find only those occurrences of the Find What text with the exact capitalization specified. For example, find the initials *USA* and not the characters *usa* in *usability*. (However, the characters *USA* in *USABILITY* will be found unless you also select the Find Whole Words Only option.)

Find Whole Words Only option

- Click the Find Whole Words Only option to find only whole-word occurrences of the Find What text. For example, find the word *men* and not the characters *men* in *mention* and *fundamental*.

Use Pattern Matching option

Special characters

- Click the Use Pattern Matching option to find strings of characters when some of the characters vary or are unknown. You can then use ? as a "wildcard," or placeholder, in the Find What edit box. You can also find special characters, such as tabs (enter ^t in the Find What edit box), and paragraph marks (enter ^p). For example, find every occurrence of a paragraph that begins with the word *Remember* by entering *^pRemember* as the Find What text. Word then looks for a paragraph mark at the end of one paragraph followed by the word *Remember* at the beginning of the next paragraph. (See the tip on the facing page for information about more complex searches using pattern matching.)

Sounds Like option

- Click the Sounds Like option to find occurrences of the Find What text that sound the same but are spelled differently.

Let's work through a find procedure using a wildcard so that you can see how they operate. Suppose you regularly confuse the two words *affect* and *effect*. You can check your use of these words in the backgrounder, as follows:

1. Press Ctrl+Home to move to the top of the document. Choose the Find command from the Edit menu, and enter *?ffect* in the Find What edit box. Then click the down arrow to the right of Down, and select All as the Search option. Click Use Pattern Matching, and then click Find Next to start the search. Word stops at the word *affects* in the second paragraph.

2. This use of *affects* is incorrect, so click Cancel to close the dialog box, and change the *a* to *e*.

3. Press Shift+F4 to repeat the search. Word stops at the word *effects*, which is correct.

4. Press Shift+F4 again to ensure that the document contains no other instances of the Find What text, and click No when Word asks whether you want to continue the search.

Replacing Text

Often, you will search a document for a series of characters with the intention of replacing them. When you suspect that you will need to make the same replacement more than a couple of times, you should use the Replace command to automate the process as much as possible. As with the Find command, using the Replace command for basic substitutions is easy.

In the earlier section about modifying AutoCorrect entries, you changed one occurrence of *National BEAT* to *USA BEAT*, leaving two occurrences of *National BEAT* unchanged. Let's find those two occurrences of the old name and replace them with the new:

1. Press Ctrl+Home to move to the beginning of the document, and then choose the Replace command from the Edit menu. Word displays the dialog box shown on the next page.

Pattern matching

By selecting the Use Pattern Matching option and constructing expressions with the operators and special characters displayed when you click the Special button, you can be very specific about the text you want to include in a search or search-and-replace operation. This kind of advanced search is beyond the scope of this book, but if you frequently perform very specific searches on lengthy documents, you might want to explore this capability further.

Notice that your settings from the Find dialog box have been applied to this dialog box, and the Find What text from the previous search is in this dialog box's Find What edit box. (You can click the down arrow to the right of the Find What edit box and select the Find What text from a list of words and phrases you have previously searched for.)

The Find What drop-down list

2. Replace the Find What text by typing *National BEAT*.

3. In the Replace With edit box, type *USA BEAT*, and press Enter. Word highlights the first occurrence of the Find What text.

4. Click Replace. Word continues the search and highlights the second occurrence.

5. Click Replace again.

6. When Word announces that it has completed the search, click OK, and then click Close to close the Replace dialog box.

As with the Find command, you can use the Match Case, Find Whole Words Only, Use Pattern Matching, and Sound Like options to refine the replace procedure. (See page 52 for more information.) To change all instances of the same word or phrase throughout a document, you can click Replace All instead of Replace. (You might want to click Replace to make one replacement first; that way you can be sure your Replace With text is correct before you make global changes.)

Checking Spelling

Even if you got all the way to the National Spelling Bee finals as a kid, you'll want to check the spelling of your documents before you expose them to the scrutiny of the outside world.

Replacing with selected text

If you want to replace text throughout a document with a block of text already contained in the document, select the text, and copy it to the Clipboard. Then choose Replace from the Edit menu, and enter the Find What text. Click an insertion point in the Replace With edit box, click the Special button, and select Clipboard Contents from the list. Then click Find Next to find the first occurrence of the Find What text, and proceed as usual.

Nothing detracts from the power of your arguments and the luster of your professional image like a typo. In the past, your readers might have overlooked the occasional misspelling. These days, running your word processor's spelling checker is so easy that readers tend to be less forgiving. The moral: Get in the habit of spell checking all your documents, especially before distributing printed copies.

You can use Word's Spelling feature to check an entire document or a block of selected text. You can check against Word's built-in dictionary or against specialized dictionaries that you create. In this section, we'll check the backgrounder.

Checking the Spelling of an Entire Document

As you created the backgrounder in this chapter, you deliberately included a few errors. Now let's see how Word for Windows handles the misspellings:

1. With the insertion point located at the top of the backgrounder, click the Spelling button on the toolbar. Word automatically begins a spelling check of the document, starting with the word containing the insertion point. When Word finds a word that is not in its dictionary, it displays this Spelling dialog box:

The dialog box's title bar tells you that by default Word uses the English (US) dictionary as its main dictionary. This dictionary can by supplemented by CUSTOM.DIC, which is empty until you add entries to it.

2. As you can see, Word stopped at the word *environmently*. Possible substitutes appear in the Suggestions list, with the closest match to the unrecognized word displayed in the

Spelling options

Clicking the Options button in the Spelling dialog box displays the Options dialog box's Spelling tab. Here you can tell Word whether you want it to suggest alternatives for the misspellings it finds and to ignore words in capital letters or that contain numbers. You can also create and select custom dictionaries (see the tip on page 57).

Change To edit box. Click the Change All button to tell Word that you want to change all occurrences of this misspelling.

3. Word continues the spelling check, stops at *GlassWorks*, and suggests *glassworks* in the Change To edit box. Click Ignore All to leave all occurrences of this name as they are.

4. Word stops at the word *dumpsters*. Although this term is not in Word's dictionary, it is correct, so click Ignore All again.

5. Next Word stops at *campaining*—another genuine misspelling. Click Change to accept Word's suggestion, *campaigning*. If Word's suggestion is not correct but one of the words in the Suggestions list is the one you want, you can select that word and then click Change. If none of the suggestions is correct, you can type the correction in the Change To edit box and then click Change. (You can also edit the word directly in the document without closing the Spelling dialog box.)

Editing Word's suggestions

6. When Word reaches the end of the document, it closes the Spelling dialog box and displays a message that the spelling check is complete. Click OK to return to your document.

Checking the Spelling of a Selection

To check the spelling of part of a document or even a single word, select the text or word, and then click the Spelling button. Word checks the selection the same way it checks an entire document, and you use the same techniques to ignore or change any words the program does not recognize.

Creating and Using Custom Dictionaries

As you have seen, you can tell Word to remember the words it should ignore during a spelling check so that it does not stumble over them if they occur later in the document. If you check the document again during the same Word session, Word won't stop for the words you told it to ignore. However, if you quit Word and check the document in a later session or if you check a different document, Word again stops for those words. That's where custom dictionaries come in handy. You can add names, technical terms, and other

Smart spelling checks

If your document contains duplicate words, such as *the the*, Word stops at the words and displays them in the Spelling window. Clicking Delete removes the duplicate word. Word also stops at strange combinations of uppercase and lowercase letters. For example, Word would stumble over *nAtional* and would suggest *national* as an appropriate substitute. To speed up the checking process, Word's suggestions generally have the same case as a misspelled word. For example, if the misspelling occurs at the beginning of a sentence and therefore starts with a capital letter, Word's suggestions also start with capital letters.

nonstandard words that you use frequently to one of these dictionaries so that Word no longer flags them every time you perform a spelling check.

Follow these steps to add a few words to CUSTOM.DIC:

1. Save the backgrounder, and choose Exit from the File menu to quit Word. Then reload the program by double-clicking its icon in Program Manager, and reload the backgrounder by choosing it from the bottom of the File menu.

2. Click the Spelling button on the toolbar to begin checking the spelling of the backgrounder.

3. When Word displays *GlassWorks* in the Spelling dialog box, click the Add button. Once the word is listed in an open custom dictionary, Word no longer treats it as a misspelling.

Adding words to dictionaries

4. When Word stops on *dumpsters*, click the Add button to add this word to the custom dictionary.

5. When Word completes the spelling check, click OK to return to your document.

You can't rely on Word's Spelling feature to identify every error in your documents. Errors of grammar, syntax, or improper word usage will pass muster in a spelling check as long as the words are spelled correctly. To catch these types of errors, you need to use Word's Grammar feature, which we discuss next.

Checking Grammar

Word's Grammar feature applies common rules to your text and identifies potential problems, suggesting corrections where appropriate and providing helpful explanations if you request them. During a grammar check, Word also checks the spelling of the document and accumulates statistics that assess its readability. Here's how to run the grammar checker on BKGROUND.DOC:

1. Be sure the insertion point is at the top of the document, and then choose Grammar from the Tools menu. The grammar

Your own dictionaries

You don't have to store words in the CUSTOM.DIC custom dictionary. You can create specialized user dictionaries for use with various kinds of documents. Choose the Spelling command from the Tools menu, and in the Spelling dialog box, click Options to display the Spelling tab of the Options dialog box. Then click New to display another dialog box, specify the name and location of the new dictionary, and click OK. Click OK again to close the Options dialog box. Then in the Spelling dialog box, click the down arrow to the right of CUSTOM.DIC to drop down a list of available dictionaries, and select the new dictionary. Now clicking the Add button will add new words to that dictionary instead of CUSTOM.DIC.

checker highlights the paragraph under *What Is Redmond BEAT?* and suggests that the word *ensure* might be confused with other words:

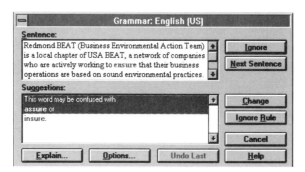

2. Click Ignore to tell Word you like the sentence the way it is.

3. Word then points out that part of the paragraph may be in the passive voice. You have used the passive voice judiciously and intentionally, so click Ignore Rule to tell Word not to check that rule anymore for this document.

4. Word next highlights a sentence under *How Does It Work?* and suggests changing the obviously incorrect *there* to *their.* Click Change. (You can also make changes directly to your document without closing the Grammar dialog box.)

5. Click Ignore for any other potential problems, until the grammar checker suggests changing *it's* to *its*, at which time click Change again. Then click Ignore for any other errors.

6. When Word finishes checking the document, it displays this Readability Statistics dialog box:

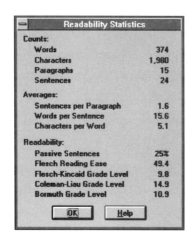

Readability statistics

The Readability Statistics dialog box displays the number of words, characters, paragraphs, and sentences in your document; the average number of sentences per paragraph, words per sentence, and characters per word; as well as an assessment of your document's readability. Readability is determined first by your use of the passive voice and then by four standard scales. Scores between 60 and 70 on the first scale and between 7 and 8 on the other three scales denote a standard writing level (seventh to eighth grade).

7. Look over these statistics, and then click OK to close the dialog box.

As you have seen, the grammar checker questions many elements of your document that are perfectly fine, and after checking a few documents, you might want to customize the Grammar program to match your writing style and the current document's tone. Unlike many grammar checkers, the program that comes with Word for Windows is very flexible. If you don't want certain rules of grammar to be applied to your writing, you have the choice of turning them off. Either click the Options button in the Grammar dialog box, or choose Options from the Tools menu and click the Grammar tab. You can then tell Word to use a different set of rules, or you can click the Customize Settings button to create your own set of rules. By default, Word uses grammar rules for business writers; selecting For Casual Writing applies fewer rules, and selecting Strictly uses all the rules. To see an explanation of a rule, highlight it in the Customize Grammar Settings dialog box and then click Explain.

Specifying grammar rules

Take the time to experiment with the grammar checker. Fake a few errors, and see whether it catches them. The program is not infallible but running it on important documents might save you from unpleasant embarrassments.

Automatic Documents:
Using Templates and Wizards

What you will learn...

Use a Word template to create an impressive press release

Start new lines without starting new paragraphs

Create classy-looking newsletters with Word's Newsletter Wizard

Redmond BEAT
14000 Leary Way, Suite 100
Redmond, WA 98052

EarthWare Wins Carson Award for "Green" Packaging

For Immediate Release

Friday, December 10, 199

Contact: Ted Lee
           Redmond BE
           555-6789

Redmond—Yesterday the Ca
Award to EarthWare Inc. Th
recycled cardboard are an
environment.

The prestigious Carson Aw
practices are environmentally
donation to the environment
Dinner on Friday March 18,

Reuse existing text whenever possible for greatest efficiency

ON THE BEAT

Volume 1 Issue 1   **December 1993**

IN THIS PREMIER ISSUE: WHO WE ARE AND WHY WE'RE HERE

Redmond Business Environmental Action Team

What is Redmond BEAT?
Redmond BEAT (Business Environmental Action Team) is a local chapter of USA BEAT, a network of companies who are actively working to ensure that their business operations are based on sound environmental practices.

How does it work?
Member companies agree to participate in two ongoing efforts: 1. They pledge to scrutinize their operations and wherever possible, implement procedures that will minimize any adverse effects on the environment. 2. They agree to field-test new "environmentally kind" products and services to evaluate their potential impact on both company costs and the environment.

When was it started?
Redmond BEAT was founded in 1989. USA BEAT, which currently has 210 local chapters, was founded in 1987.

Why was it started?
The chartering of Redmond BEAT was spearheaded by long-time Redmond resident William Henry, President of Creative GlassWorks. Struck by the incongruity between his family's efforts to recycle household waste and the fact that his company was sending several dumpsters of garbage to the Redmond landfill every month, Henry began looking for other ways to dispose of the packaging in which his company received raw materials. His questions caused one of his suppliers, Jordan Manufacturing, to explore alternative packaging methods. The result was less garbage in the Creative GlassWorks dumpsters at no additional cost and negligible other effects for either company. In the meantime, Henry learned about USA BEAT, and a few months of persuasive campaigning later, Redmond BEAT became the newest chapter of a rapidly growing national association.

Who can join?
Membership in Redmond BEAT is open to all companies licensed to do business in the city of Redmond.

Why should my company join?
Current members cite two main reasons for joining. Many companies are managed by people who were attracted to this area by its natural beauty and who want to be part of the effort to preserve it. Other companies stress the potential advantages in today's competitive markets of being perceived as a "green" company by consumers who are increasingly environmentally aware.

How can I find out more?
Come to a meeting. Redmond BEAT meets at 8:00 AM on the last Tuesday of every month in the Community Center. For more information, contact Ted Lee at 555-6789.

Control where columns break for a balanced professional look

C hapters 1 and 2 introduced you to Word for Windows and the basic techniques you can use to create and edit documents. If you didn't learn any more about Word than the material covered in those chapters, you could probably produce most of the documents you need. Of course, you could probably use a bicycle to get to most of the places you need to go, too. Just as there are faster and more convenient ways to travel, there are faster and more convenient ways to create documents.

With Word, you don't have to struggle to create attractive documents, such as letters, memos, newsletters, brochures, invoices, calendars, and even full-size books. In this chapter, we look at templates and wizards, which can practically create a document for you.

Using Word's Templates

Template basics

A Word for Windows template is a pattern that contains the information, formatting, AutoText entries, styles, and macros that are used in a particular type of document. All Word for Windows documents are based on a template: When you click the New button on the toolbar to create a new document, that document is based on the Normal template. Word comes with quite a few other templates that you can use as is or modify; or you can create your own templates (see page 114). To create a new document based on a template other than Normal, you use the New command on the File menu. You then save the file as a regular Word document. The template remains on disk in its original state, ready to be used as the basis for another document. Using templates is kind of like buying preprinted forms and then filling in the blanks, except that you can design and redesign the form at any time.

The TEMPLATE directory

As part of the standard installation procedure for Word for Windows, a number of sample templates were copied to your WINWORD\TEMPLATE directory. To see a list of these templates and a brief explanation of each one, simply follow these steps:

1. Choose the New command from the File menu to display this dialog box:

If the sample templates are installed on your hard disk, the Template list offers a variety of templates on which to base the new document. The default selection (which is available even when the sample templates have not been installed) is Normal. Selecting this template opens a blank document and displays the standard menus. Selecting a wizard walks you through the steps of setting up a more complex template (see page 72.

The Normal template

Wizards

2. Click the Agenda Wizard once to highlight it. Notice that the Description box at the bottom of the dialog box displays a short description of the highlighted item.

3. Press the Down Arrow key to scroll down through the list, reading the description of each item.

As you can tell from their names and descriptions, the sample templates provide the basis for many common business documents. For example, in Chapter 1 you created a letter while becoming familiar with Word's basic features. You could also have used one of the letter templates supplied with Word as the basis for the letter.

The Press Release Template

Word for Windows provides three versions of a press release: a classical format named Presrel1, a contemporary format named Presrel2, and a format that emulates the output of a typewriter named Presrel3. All three provide a structure into which you plug the same information. Take a look at the classical press release by following the steps on the next page.

The Normal template

Word's Normal template, which is stored in a file called NORMAL.DOT in the WINWORD\TEMPLATE directory, contains all global styles, AutoText entries, macros, and key/menu assignments predefined by Word or created by you. These global elements are available for all documents you create, no matter which template they are based on. If you mess up your NORMAL.DOT file, you can restore the original file by deleting the current NORMAL.DOT or by renaming it. Word then creates a new file the next time you start the program. (Of course, you lose any global elements you added to the old NORMAL.DOT.)

1. Highlight Presrel1 in the Template list, and either press Enter or click OK. Instead of the usual blank document, Word displays this document on your screen:

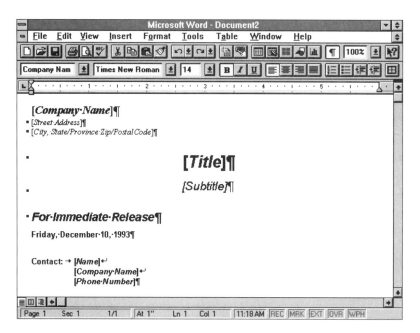

As you can see, all the common elements of a press release have placeholders within square brackets, and Word has entered the current date (using the date stored in your computer). Let's go ahead and fill in the press release now. In the steps below, select the words indicated but not the paragraph mark following the words. (If paragraph marks are not visible on your screen, simply click the Show/Hide ¶ button on the toolbar to turn them on. If the ruler is not displayed, choose Ruler from the View menu to turn it on.) Word stores the formatting for each paragraph in its paragraph mark, and deleting a paragraph mark deletes the formatting. If you ax a paragraph mark by mistake, click the Undo button on the toolbar immediately to reinstate it.

1. Select *[Company Name]*, and then replace it by typing *Redmond BEAT*.

2. Replace *[Street Address]* with *14000 Leary Way, Suite 100*, and replace the placeholders for the city, state, and ZIP code with *Redmond, WA 98052*.

Date fields

Word automatically enters the date stored by your system's clock/calendar when you open a document based on the press release template. Why? Because the document contains a special code called a *field*. Fields can contain a variety of information; this particular field is an instruction to get the current date and display it in the field's location. If you do nothing to this field, Word will insert the current date each time you print the document. If you want to "freeze" the current date, click the field to select it, and then press Ctrl+Shift+F9. The field is converted to normal text that will not be updated and that can be edited. To insert a date field in your document, choose Date And Time from the Insert menu, and in the Date And Time dialog box, select a date format, click the Insert As Field option to select it, and then click OK.

3. Replace *[Title]* with *EarthWare Wins Carson Award for "Green" Packaging*, and then delete *[Subtitle]* and its paragraph mark.

4. Replace *[Name]* with *Ted Lee*, *[Company Name]* with *Redmond BEAT*, and *[Phone Number]* with *555-6789*.

Take a moment to admire your work. Without adding any formatting of your own, you've created a professional-looking header for a press release. But that title could use some fine-tuning. It would be better balanced if the line break occurred after *Award* instead of after *"Green."* Let's fix that now:

1. Click an insertion point to the left of *for*, and press Enter. Oops! That doesn't look so good. You need a way of breaking the line without adding all that extra space.

2. Click the Undo button.

3. Now hold down the Shift key, and press Enter. That's better: ←

Inserting a line break

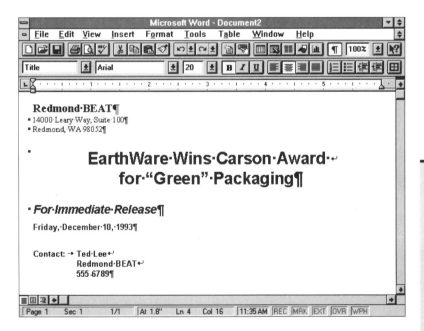

Pressing Shift+Enter inserts a line break at the insertion point without starting a new paragraph. The line break is indicated on your screen by the broken arrow after *Award*.

Why pressing Enter inserts so much space

Pressing Enter to break the title into two lines creates a new paragraph that has all the formatting of the original paragraph, including space above it to set it off from the preceding element in the press release. You can adjust the spacing between paragraphs using the Paragraph command on the Format menu. See page 105 for more information.

4. Save the document with the name PRESSREL.DOC.

Below the press release header, you need to enter the text of the press release. This information is essentially the same as that contained in the letter you wrote in Chapter 1. The beauty of a word processor like Word is that instead of retyping the information, you can borrow it from the letter and edit it to suit the purpose of the press release. Here's how:

1. Press Ctrl+End to move to the end of the document, press Ctrl+Backspace several times to delete *[Type information here]*, and replace *[City]* with *Redmond*.

2. Now click the Open button on the toolbar, and in the Open dialog box, double-click PI_AWARD.DOC to open the letter from Chapter 1 in its own window.

Resizing a window

3. Choose Arrange All from the Window menu to display both windows, with the letter in the top one and the press release in the bottom one. Then point to the bottom border of the top window (below the horizontal scroll bar). When the pointer changes to a double arrow, drag the border down until the letter's window fills three-quarters of the screen, but *Redmond* is still visible in the bottom window, like this:

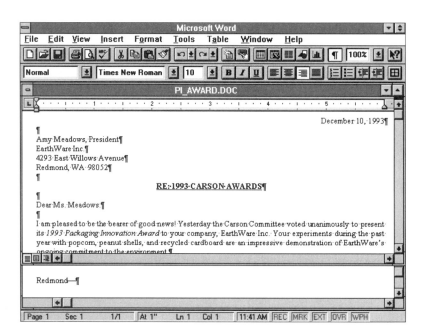

4. Scroll the letter in its window until you can see its text, and then select the two paragraphs, including the paragraph mark between them.

5. With the pointer over the selection, hold down the left mouse button, drag the shadow insertion point between the dash and the paragraph mark after *Redmond* in the other window, and release the mouse button.

6. Activate the letter's window, choose Close from the File menu, and click No when Word asks whether you want to save your changes to the document.

7. Click the press release window's Maximize button to expand the window, which looks like this:

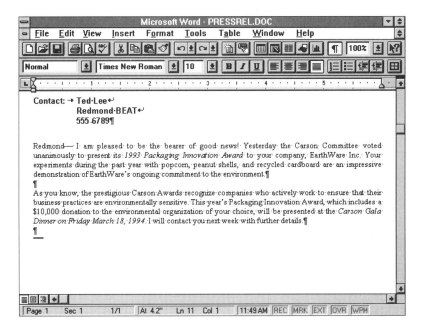

8. After you make a few changes, the press release will be ready to send out to the media. Edit the text of the press release so that it looks like the one shown on the next page.

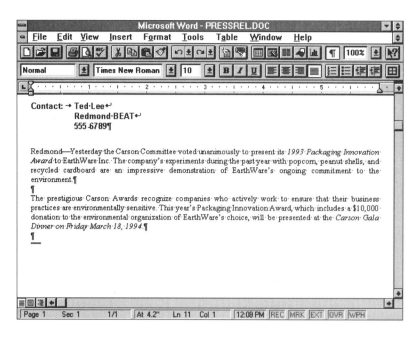

9. Now save and print the document, and then close it.

The Invoice Template

The press release templates are pretty simple, containing only some formatted text and a date field. For an example of a more complex template, let's take a look at the invoice template:

1. Choose New from the File menu, and double-click Invoice in the Template list. Word displays this document:

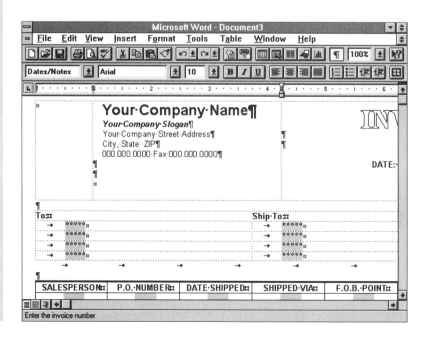

Word forms

The Invoice template is an example of a Word form. To create a similar form, which can be as simple as an expense report or as complex as an insurance form, you use the Forms toolbar to set up a template with areas called *form fields*. These fields can be text, check boxes, or drop-down lists. You then click the Protect Form button on the Forms toolbar to protect the template so that only the form fields can be changed. When you create a new document based on a form template, you can fill in the form on the computer by using the Tab, Enter, or Arrow keys to move from field to field.

The invoice template creates a special type of Word document, known as a *form*, that is protected so that you can enter and change only the information in specific fields. If you scroll to the right, you'll see that the gray area after INVOICE NO is dark, indicating that it is the active field. Notice also that the status bar displays an instruction about what information you should enter in the active field.

Forms

2. Press Tab. The active field moves to the next item you are allowed to edit—the first line of the To section.

3. Press Tab several more times, noting the instructions in the status bar, until you reach the first entry in the Quantity column. Notice that the status bar displays an instruction to enter the number of units purchased.

4. Type *3*, and press Tab twice to move to the Unit Price column.

5. Type *5.27*, and press Tab again. Then scroll the window so that you can see the Amount column, where the total amount, $15.81, has been calculated:

Automatic calculations

Word math

The invoice is actually a table, and Word performs the calculations in the invoice by means of formulas that are constructed using the Formula command on the Table menu. By designating the columns of the table as letters (A, B, C, and so on) and the rows of the table as numbers (1, 2, 3, and so on), Word can identify the contents of a particular column and row for use in calculations. As a result, you can construct simple formulas such as $=A1+B1$ and $=A1*B1$ (where * designates multiplication, and / designates division). Or you can use built-in Word functions to perform common calculations such as summing or averaging a column or row of numbers (see page 131).

6. Scroll down to the subtotal and total due fields, which word has also calculated for you.

If an invoice of this nature is useful to you, you can modify the template so that it displays your company name and address, and other pertinent information. Try this:

1. Choose Close from the File menu, and click No to discard your edits.

Opening a template file

2. Click the Open button on the toolbar, and in the Open dialog box, click the down arrow to the right of the List Files Of Type option in the bottom-left corner, and select Document Templates from the drop-down list.

3. In the Directories list, double-click the TEMPLATE directory icon to display the list of files stored in the WINWORD\TEMPLATE directory, like this:

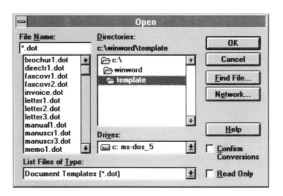

The DOT extension

Each template file has a DOT extension that identifies it as a template, and for a template to appear in the New dialog box's default Template list, it must be stored in the WINWORD\ TEMPLATE directory.

4. Double-click INVOICE.DOT to display the invoice template's file.

Modifying a template

5. Before you go any further, use the Save As command to save the template file with the name *red_inv.dot* so that any changes you make will not affect the original file. (In the Save As dialog box, check that the Save File As Type setting is Document Template before clicking OK.)

Now let's make the necessary changes:

1. Try clicking an insertion point in *Your Company Name*. The insertion point jumps to the INVOICE NO field. You can't change anything in the template except the entries designated by gray shading because the document is protected.

2. Choose Unprotect Document from the Tools menu.

Removing document protection

3. Delete the entire *Your Company Slogan* line, and then change the name, address, and phone number as shown here, being careful to retain the paragraph marks:

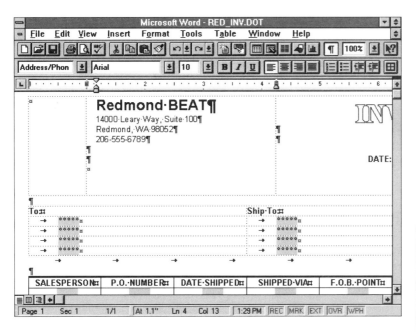

Document protection

Word offers several types of document protection. In addition to protecting all but the fields of a form, you can protect a document from changes by other people but allow them to annotate, or add comments to, the document by selecting the Annotations option in the Protect Document dialog box. You can allow changes to the document but tell Word to keep track of the changes by selecting the Revisions option. And you can assign a password of up to 15 characters that must be entered before Word will unprotect a document. (Passwords are case-sensitive.)

4. Choose Protect Document from the Tools menu, click the Forms option to allow changes only in form fields, and then click OK.

5. Finally, click the Save button on the toolbar to save your changes, and then close the template.

6. To test your new template, choose New from the File menu, scroll down the Template list, and double-click Red_inv to display a document based on the modified Invoice template. Then close the document.

   You can use this same basic procedure to change other Word templates to suit your needs.

Using Word's Wizards

The Invoice template is fairly complex, but all that's involved is the form you see when you create a new document based on the template. When you create a new document based on a wizard, the document you see depends on your answers to questions the wizard asks. Microsoft includes a variety of wizards with Word, and other people will undoubtedly develop wizard packages in the future. (The creation of wizards requires programming expertise and is beyond the scope of this book; however, you can create your own wizards if you are willing to put in the effort.)

Wizard basics

Wizards typically consist of two parts: the user interface, which solicits the information needed to customize the template; and the program that does the actual customizing. Each part can vary from straightforward to pretty complex, depending on the sophistication of the template the wizard creates. Let's take a look at a fairly simple wizard that creates a calendar in one of several designs.

The Calendar Wizard

The Calendar Wizard creates calendars for up to a ten-year period for any years between January 1900 and December 4095. For a demonstration, follow these steps:

Creating a calendar

1. Start the wizard by choosing New from the File menu and double-clicking Calendar Wizard in the Template list. As the wizard is being loaded, watch the status bar, which displays short messages telling you what is happening. After a few moments, this dialog box appears on your screen:

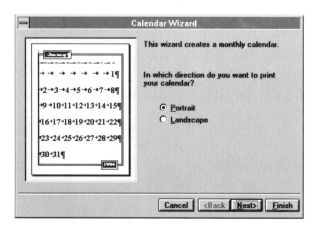

The design of this user interface is typical: Option buttons allow you to specify choices that determine the appearance or function of the template; a picture shows you the result of your choice; and the buttons at the bottom of the dialog box allow you to complete this step in the process and move forward to the next step or back to the previous step. Normally, each step has a default selection, so you can create the standard version of the template—in this case, a calendar—by simply clicking the Next button at each step. Or you can click Finish at any step to create the template using the default selections for the remaining steps.

The wizard's user interface

2. Click Landscape, and then click Next.

3. Click Next again to accept the default Boxes And Borders option, and then click Next again to specify no picture.

4. In the fourth dialog box, specify *1994* as the year (in both Year edit boxes), and then click Finish to display the calendar.

5. Click the Zoom Control's down arrow, and select Whole Page from the drop-down list. The calendar is displayed in page layout view, like this:

Viewing the entire page

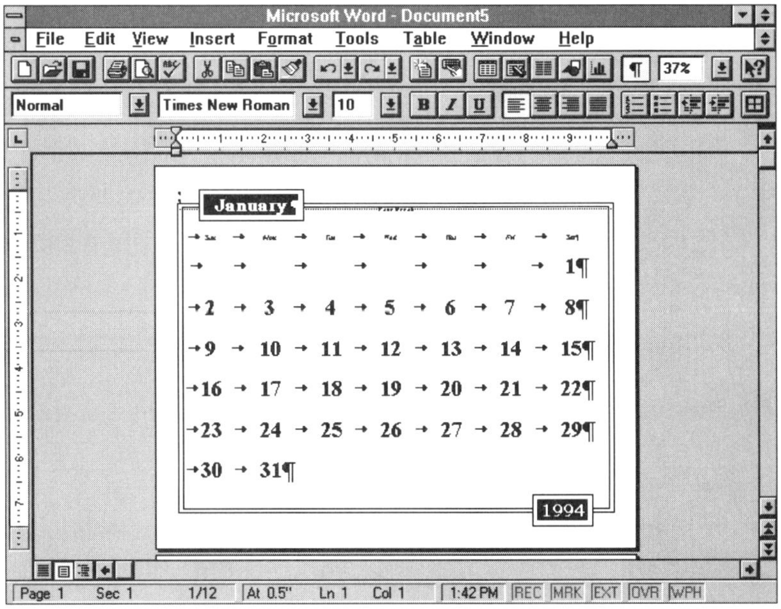

6. Press PageDown to page through each month of the calendar.

> **One-month calendar**
>
> To print a calendar for only one month, set the starting and ending dates to the same month. For example, to print a calendar for March 1994, select March from both the Start and End drop-down lists.

Printing the calendar

7. If you want, print the calendar just as you would any Word document, and save it with the name CALENDAR.DOC. (If necessary, double-click the WINWORD directory in the Save As dialog box to store the file in that directory.)

8. Close the calendar document so that we can look at another wizard.

Word macros

If you find that you often repeat a series of commands when working with Word documents, you can record those commands and save them as a macro. To create a macro, simply choose Macro from the Tools menu, and click the Record button. A dialog box appears in which you name the macro; assign it to a toolbar, menu, or shortcut key combination; attach it to a template; type a description; and click OK. The pointer acquires a tape cassette icon indicating that you are recording, and the Macro Record toolbar appears on the screen. Now perform the steps necessary to carry out the desired action. When you finish, click the Stop button on the Macro Record toolbar. Behind the scenes, Word has created a program in WordBasic, a fairly simple but powerful programming language. You can view the program by choosing Macro from the Tools menu, selecting the macro you just recorded, and clicking Edit. (When you finish viewing the macro, you can close it like any normal Word document.) Run the macro by choosing Macro, selecting the macro's name, and clicking Run or by pressing the shortcut key combination.

The Award Wizard

In this section, we'll use the Award Wizard to create a certificate for EarthWare's packaging innovation award. As you'll see, this wizard allows you to play an active role in the design of the certificate. Here are the steps:

1. Choose New from the File menu, and double-click Award Wizard in the Template list. Word displays this dialog box:

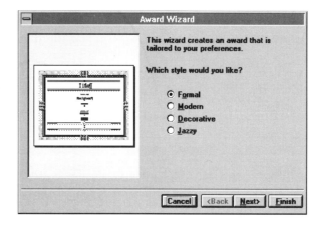

2. You are offered a choice of four styles for the award. If you want, select each one to see a small picture of it, but be sure to end up with Modern selected, and then click Next.

3. Select Portrait and No, and then click Next.

The next few dialog boxes ask you for information that is in the letter you wrote in Chapter 1. Normally, you would simply open the document and copy the information. However, you are currently running a wizard program within Word, and you won't be able to access the Word menus until you finish the program. But provided your computer has enough memory, there is a way you can open the letter. Follow these steps to start another instance of Word:

1. Press Alt+Tab until Program Manager is active, double-click the Microsoft Word icon to start a second instance of Word, and then click the Open button and open PI_AWARD.DOC.

   Opening a second instance of Word

2. Select *EarthWare Inc.* in the address at the top of the letter, and press Ctrl+C to copy the selection to the Clipboard.

3. Press Alt+Tab until the version of Word that is running the Award Wizard becomes active.

4. If *Recipient* is not already selected, press Alt+T to select it. (Notice that the letter *T* in *Type the name* is underlined, indicating that you can press Alt+T to select the information in that edit box.)

5. Press Ctrl+V to paste the name from the Clipboard, replacing the selected text.

6. Press Alt+Tab to move back to the other instance of Word, copy *1993 Packaging Innovation Award* to the Clipboard, press Alt+Tab to return to the Award Wizard, press Alt+A to select the information in the second edit box, and press Ctrl+V to paste the copied text. Then click Next.

   Switching between Word programs

7. The wizard asks you to provide the names of the people presenting the award and may suggest a name. Type *Ted Lee* in the edit box, and click the Add button to add that name to the list of signatures that will appear on the certificate. Then click Next.

8. Select the Presented By option, and in the edit box, type *The Carson Committee*, and click Next.

9. In the next dialog box, press Alt+D to select the date, press Alt+Tab to move to the other instance of Word, copy *Friday March 18, 1994*, press Alt+Tab to return to the Award Wizard, and press Ctrl+V. Repeat these steps for the additional text, pressing Alt+T to highlight the existing text, pressing Alt+Tab to move to the letter, copying *EarthWare's ongoing commitment to the environment*, pressing Alt+Tab to move back to the Award Wizard, and pasting the text into the additional text edit box. Then click Next.

10. You have now provided all the information that the wizard requires, but before clicking Finish, return to the second instance of Word, and choose Exit from the File menu. Otherwise, your computer may run out of memory while the wizard is creating the certificate. Then click Finish. The wizard creates a new document, enters the information you have provided, and formats it all in an appropriate manner for the style of certificate you specified. Here's the result:

Closing the second
instance of Word

Creating and removing text boxes

The gray areas in the award certificate are text boxes created with Word's drawing program. You create a text box when you want text to appear in a specific location on the page, regardless of what else might be on the page. To insert a text box, right-click the toolbar, choose Drawing from the shortcut menu to display the Drawing toolbar, click the Text Box button (the sixth one from the left), and drag the cross-hair pointer to create a box. You can then click an insertion point in the text box and type and format your text using normal techniques. To remove a text box, move the pointer to any edge of the text box, and when a four-headed arrow appears below the pointer, click to select the box. Then you can press Delete or choose Clear from the Edit menu to delete the text box.

Nothing says that you have to accept the certificate the way it comes. As a matter of fact, with the long title we provided, you can see that a little editing is in order. Here's how to clean up the title:

1. Click any word in the title three times to select the entire paragraph containing the title.

2. Click the down arrow to the right of the Font Size box, and select 28 from the drop-down list.

3. The certificate is a normal Word document that you can edit any way you want. You can expand on any of the text or totally delete sections you don't need. For example, we added a few blank paragraphs in strategic spots to center the text entries in their shaded areas, like this:

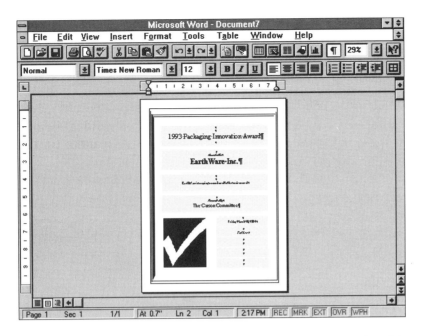

4. After experimenting with this document a little, save it with the name AWARD.DOC, print it, and close it.

The Newsletter Wizard

As a grand finale, let's take a look at the wizard for creating newsletters:

1. Choose New from the File menu, and double-click Newslttr Wizard in the Template list to display this first dialog box:

Creating a three-column newsletter

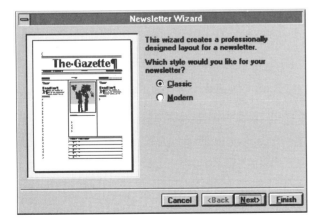

2. Click Next to accept the default Classic option, and then click Next again to set up a newsletter with three columns.

3. Press Alt+T, type *ON THE BEAT* as the name of the newsletter, and click Next.

4. Click Next to specify that the newsletter will contain 2 pages.

5. Click the check boxes for Table Of Contents and Fancy First Letters to deselect those options, and then with Date and Volume And Issue still selected, click Next.

6. Click Finish to display the newsletter template in page layout view, like this:

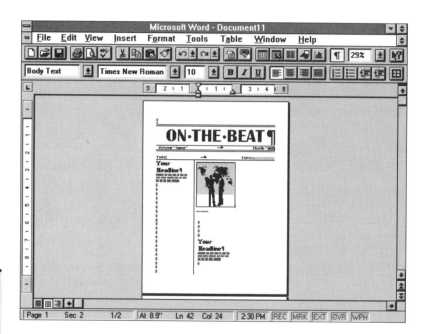

Fancy first letters

You can add fancy first letters, called *dropped capital letters*, to any paragraph of any document. Simply click an insertion point in the paragraph you want to begin with a fancy first letter, and choose Drop Cap from the Format menu. In the Drop Cap dialog box, select either Dropped or In Margin as the Position setting, select a font, and specify how many lines you want the letter to span and the space between the letter and the following text. Click OK, and then click Yes to switch to page layout view so that you can see the letter.

Now you're ready to create the first issue of your newsletter:

1. Click the down arrow to the right of the Zoom Control box on the toolbar, and select 100% from the drop-down list. Then press Ctrl+Home.

2. Scroll the window to the right until you can see the date, select *Month*, and type the current month.

3. Scroll back to the left, click an insertion point to the left of the *T* in the first *TOPIC*, hold down the Shift key, scroll to the right, and click between the *C* of the second *TOPIC* and the paragraph mark. Release the Shift key. Then press CapsLock, and type *IN THIS PREMIER ISSUE: WHO WE ARE AND*

WHY WE'RE HERE. Turn off CapsLock. Now click the Center button on the Formatting toolbar to center the new topic line.

4. Click the picture, and press Delete to remove it. Then choose Frame from the Format menu, and click Remove Frame at the bottom of the Frame dialog box. (We discuss this dialog box in greater detail on page 122.)

Removing the picture and frame

5. Select and delete the paragraph that begins *Replace this text* under the first *Your Headline* heading.

6. Save the newsletter with the name NEWSBEAT.DOC.

Well, you're ready to tackle the main text of the newsletter. The information you want to present is the same as that in the backgrounder you wrote in Chapter 2. You certainly don't want to retype the information, so we'll take this opportunity to demonstrate one way to locate the existing backgrounder file and incorporate it in the newsletter.

Finding Files

When you saved the backgrounder in Chapter 2, you filled in a Summary Info dialog box with information that described the file. When we first discussed the Summary Info dialog box, we explained that this extra step might save you time later if you needed to locate the file. Now you have the opportunity to put the information in this dialog box to use.

Suppose you have written not a handful but two hundred documents, and you now need to locate the Redmond BEAT backgrounder so that you can include it in the first issue of your newsletter. Did you call the file REDBEAT.DOC or RED_BACK.DOC? And which directory did you store it in? Fortunately, with Word's Find File command you can find files without knowing their exact names and locations. The Find File command is available on the File menu, or you can access its dialog box by clicking the Find File button in the Open dialog box. Try this:

1. Click the Open button on the toolbar, and then click the Find File button to display a dialog box similar to the one shown on the next page.

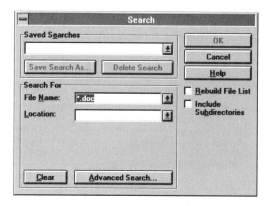

2. If Word has already performed any searches and if you saved the search specifications, you can retrieve them and run that search again. But you want to run a new search, so click the Advanced Search button to display this dialog box:

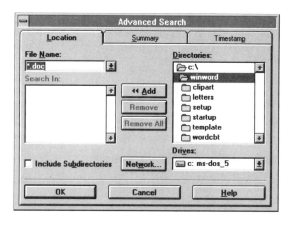

Searching on extension, drive, and directory

You use the options on the Location tab to refine a search by specifying the extension to search for and the drives and directories to be searched. The object is to specify only as much information as is needed to find the desired files.

Specifying a directory

3. Click C:\ in the Directories list, and click the Add button to add C:\ to the Search In list to the left. Then click the Include Subdirectories option to select it. So far, you have specified that you want to search your entire hard disk for files with the DOC extension.

Searching on summary information

4. Click the Summary tab to display these options:

You use these options to limit the search results to files that have specific information in their Summary Info dialog boxes.

5. In the Subject edit box, type *Backgrounder*, and then click OK twice to close the Advanced Search and Search dialog boxes and start the search. Word searches the Summary Info dialog boxes of the files with the DOC extension for entries that match the criteria you have specified. It then displays this Find File dialog box, with the names of matching files—in this case, BKGROUND.DOC—in the Listed Files list and the document itself in the Preview Of box:

Specifying subject information

Search results

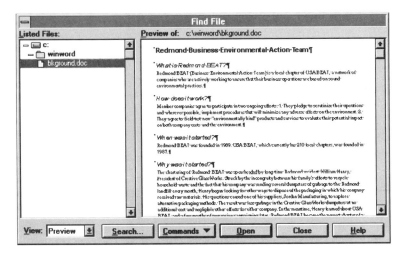

Depending on how many files you have on your hard disk and the way you perform a search, you may locate exactly the file you need right off the bat, or you may end up with a list of files. Before opening a file for editing or printing, you can have a quick look at its contents or other information about it

Other Find File options

To save the criteria used for a file search so that you can repeat the search later, click the Save Search As button, and type a name for the search. Delete a previously saved set of search criteria by selecting the search and clicking the Delete Search button. Build a new list of files in the Find File dialog box by simply clicking the Rebuild File List check box. In the Advanced Search dialog box, you can use the Summary tab to search for documents that contain specific text as well as specific Summary Info entries, and you can use the Timestamp tab to search for files revised or created during specific time periods.

File viewing options →

directly in the Find File dialog box. The contents of this dialog box are controlled by the setting of the View option in the bottom-left corner. If View is set to Preview, as it is here, then the actual contents of the file are displayed in the box to the right. If View is set to Summary, then the summary information for the file that is highlighted in the list of files is displayed. If View is set to File Info, then a variety of information about all the files in the list (rather than only the selected file) is displayed.

Find File dialog box options →

Having located the correct file, you can use the Commands button to open (as read-only), print, delete, or copy it from the Find File dialog box. If this dialog box displays more than one file, you can perform any of these operations on several files at once by first selecting them. You can also change their summary information and sort them. Here, we'll show you how to open the backgrounder file. Follow this simple step:

Opening a file from the Find File dialog box →

1. With BKGROUND.DOC selected in the Find File dialog box, click the Open button. Word first closes the Find File dialog box and then opens BKGROUND.DOC in its own window.

Completing the Newsletter

Now let's merge the backgrounder with the newsletter:

Copying one document into another →

1. Select the entire text of the backgrounder by triple-clicking in the selection area to the left of the text, click the Copy button on the toolbar, and then choose Close from the File menu to close the file.

2. With the insertion point in the paragraph immediately following the *Your Headline* paragraph, click the Paste button to insert the backgrounder in the newsletter.

All that's left is a little more fine-tuning:

1. Delete *Your Headline* (but not its paragraph mark).

2. Select *Redmond Business Environmental Action Team* (but not its paragraph mark), and use drag-and-drop editing to move the selection to the paragraph above. The heading is instantly reformatted according to the specifications stored in the headline paragraph mark.

3. The word *Environmental* breaks badly, so with the headline still highlighted, select 22 from the Font Size drop-down list on the Formatting toolbar to make the characters of the headline a little smaller.

4. Delete the blank paragraph below the headline.

5. Now delete all the extraneous information at the bottom of the document. The quickest way is to click an insertion point at the beginning of the blank paragraph below the telephone number, press F8 to turn on Extend-Selection mode, press Ctrl+End to select all the text from the insertion point to the end of the document, and then press Delete.

6. Even out the columns by clicking an insertion point at the beginning of the *When was it started?* heading at the bottom of the first column, choosing Break from the Insert menu, selecting Column Break, and then clicking OK. Repeat this step to insert a column break before the *Who can join?* heading at the bottom of the second column.

Inserting column breaks

7. Click the Print Preview button to see these results:

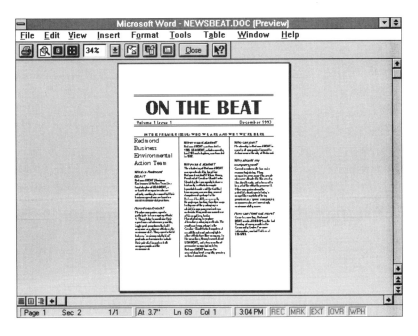

8. Safeguard the file by clicking the Save button on the toolbar. Then print the newsletter, which should look like the one at the beginning of the chapter.

Eye-Catching Documents: Creating a Flyer

What you will learn...

Set first line indents and the space above and below paragraphs

EarthWare Wins Carson Award for "Green" Packaging

Yesterday the Carson Committee[1] voted unanimously to present its *1993 Packaging Innovation Award* to EarthWare Inc. The company's experiments during the past year with popcorn, peanut shells, and recycled cardboard are an impressive demonstration of EarthWare's ongoing commitment to the environment.

The prestigious Carson Awards recognize companies who actively work to ensure that their business practices are environmentally sensitive. This year's Packaging Innovation Award, which includes a $10,000 donation to the environmental organization of EarthWare's choice, will be presented at the *Carson Gala Dinner on Friday March 18, 1994.*

REDMOND BUSINESS ENVIRONMENTAL ACTION TEAM

Dress up headings with borders and shading

Turn formatting combinations into styles

What is Redmond BEAT?

Redmond BEAT (Business Environmental Action Team) is a local chapter of USA BEAT, a network of companies who are actively working to ensure that their business operations are based on sound environmental practices.

How does it work?

Member companies agree to participate in two ongoing efforts:

Click a button to create numbered and bulleted lists

1. They pledge to scrutinize their operations and wherever possible, implement procedures that will minimize any adverse effects on the environment.

2. They agree to field-test new "environmentally kind" products and services to evaluate their potential impact on both company costs and the environment.

When was it started?

Redmond BEAT was founded in 1989. USA BEAT, which currently has 210 local chapters, was founded in 1987.

Why was it started?

The chartering of Redmond BEAT was spearheaded by long-time Redmond resident William Henry, President of Creative GlassWorks. Struck by the incongruity between his family's efforts to recycle household waste and the fact that his company was sending several dumpsters of garbage to the Redmond landfill every month, Henry began looking for other ways to dispose of the packaging in which his company received raw materials. His questions caused one of his suppliers, Jordan Manufacturing, to explore alternative packaging methods. The result was less garbage in the Creative GlassWorks dumpsters at no additional cost and negligible other effects for either company. In the meantime, Henry learned about USA BEAT, and a few months of persuasive campaigning later, Redmond BEAT became the newest chapter of a rapidly growing national association.

Who can join?

Membership in Redmond BEAT is open to all companies licensed to do business in the city of Redmond.

Why should my company join?

Current members cite two main reasons for joining. Many companies are managed by people who were attracted to this area by its natural beauty and who want to be a part of the effort to preserve it. Other companies stress the potential advantages in today's competitive markets of being perceived as a "green" company by consumers who are increasingly environmentally aware.

Use multicolumn formats to vary document designs

How can I find out more?

Come to a meeting. Redmond BEAT meets at 8:00 AM on the last Tuesday of every month in the Community Center. For more information, contact Ted Lee at 555-6789.

---

[1] Author of *The Silent Spring*, an apocryphal vision of the results of people's thoughtless manipulation of the environment for their own short-term needs, Rachel Carson was a revered pioneer environmentalist.

Create headers and footers to carry repeating information

Use footnotes for references and tangential information

Everybody has their own style—that special something that sets them apart from others. For some people it is the way they dress; for others it is the way they walk, talk, hold their head, or any combination of physical, mental, and emotional attributes. Likewise, different types of documents have different styles—that particular combination of formatting that allows us to quickly distinguish a newspaper clipping from a memo.

As you've seen, Word makes it easy to create a variety of documents with distinctive styles. Some of you may find that the set of predefined documents provided by Word's templates and Wizards meets all your needs. But what happens if the document you have in mind doesn't quite fit any of the predefined formats? For those occasions, you need to know how to manipulate a document's formatting so that you can achieve the effect you want.

In this chapter, we show you how to combine the backgrounder from Chapter 2 and the press release from Chapter 3 to create a flyer. We explore several basic formatting techniques, show you how to turn combinations of formats into styles that you can apply with a couple of clicks of the mouse button, and then describe the procedure for creating custom templates to add to Word's predefined set. As you have seen in previous chapters, a well-designed document uses formatting to provide visual cues about its structure. For example, a report might use large bold type for first-level headings and smaller bold type for second-level headings. Summary paragraphs might be indented and italic. We'll keep in mind the principals of good design in this chapter. But

Formatting with caution →

before we proceed, here's a word of warning: When it comes to formatting, use restraint. We don't want to stifle the truly creative among you—in the hands of a skilled designer, the innovative juxtaposition of different styles can produce dynamite results. However, the rest of us are just as likely to produce visual disasters. In the business world, it's better for your documents to err on the conservative side, using tried-and-true combinations and adhering to basic principles of balance and good taste, than to break new ground and risk appearing amateurish or frivolous.

To create the sample flyer, we'll start by merging the back-grounder and press release files and then get to work on formatting the flyer. Follow these steps:

1. Starting with a blank screen, click the Open button on the toolbar. When the Open dialog box is displayed, double-click BKGROUND.DOC to open it.

2. To safeguard the original backgrounder file, choose Save As from the File menu, and change the name of the version now on your screen to FLYER.DOC.

3. Press Ctrl+Home to be sure that the insertion point is at the top of the document, and choose File from the Insert menu to display the File dialog box.

Merging documents

4. Select PRESSREL.DOC from the File Name list box, and click OK to merge the file with FLYER.DOC.

5. Press Ctrl+Home to move to the top of the combined document, and select and delete everything from the press release except the title and the two paragraphs (don't forget the two blank paragraphs). Also select and delete *Redmond* and the dash at the beginning of the first paragraph.

6. Click the Save button on the toolbar to save the combined document, which should look like this:

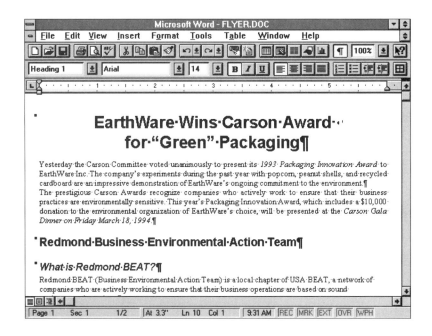

From now on, we won't tell you when to save the flyer, but you should do so at regular intervals to safeguard your work.

Making Titles Stand Out

As you know, you apply character formatting when you want to change the appearance of individual characters. Here we'll focus on the titles of the two "articles" in the new flyer, and we'll use the Formatting toolbar as well as the Font command to control the way the titles look. Let's get started:

1. Move to the top of the document, select the title of the press release, change the font to Times New Roman, and change the size to 16 points. Then delete the line break so that the title is all on one line.

2. Now select *Redmond Business Environmental Action Team*, the title of the backgrounder. Click the Center button on the Formatting toolbar to center the title, and then change the font to Times New Roman and the size to 18 points.

3. Right-click the selected title, and choose Font from the short-cut menu. Word displays this dialog box:

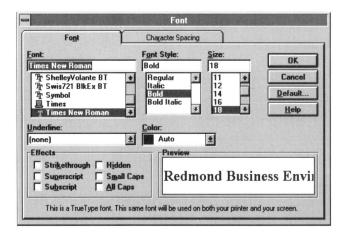

As you can see, the dialog box reflects the character formatting of the selected title. It also provides several formatting options not available on the Formatting toolbar.

4. Click Small Caps in the Effects section to format the title in small capital letters with large initial capital letters, and then click OK.

Painting formats

If you want to format a block of text with a set of formats that you have already applied to another block of text, you can copy all the formatting in a simple three-step procedure. Select the text whose formats you want to copy, click the Format Painter button on the toolbar, and then select the text you want to format. Word duplicates the formatting for the new selection.

If you want, you can experiment with some of the other options in the Font dialog box before moving on.

Adding Borders and Shading

To add emphasis to particular paragraphs, you can draw lines above and below or to the left and right of them, or you can surround the paragraphs with different styles of boxes. Let's box the backgrounder title:

1. Click the Borders button on the Formatting toolbar to display the Borders toolbar between the Formatting toolbar and the ruler, like this:

Displaying the Borders toolbar

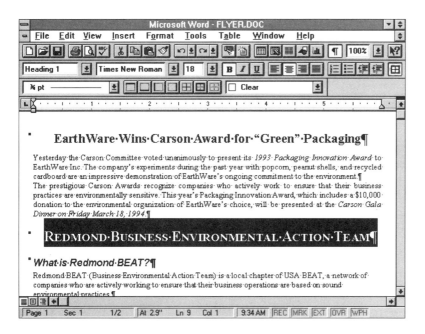

You might want to take a moment to display the names and descriptions of the buttons on the Borders toolbar.

2. With the backgrounder title still selected, click the Outside Border button. Word draws a box around the title.

Adding a border

3. Click the down arrow to the right of the Line Style box, and select the 1 1/2 pt single-line option.

Changing the line style

4. Next click the down arrow to the right of the Shading box, and then select 25% to fill the box around the title with a gray color that is made up of 25 percent black dots and 75 percent white dots.

Adding shading

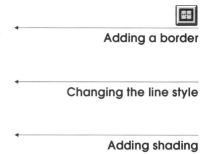

5. Click anywhere to remove the highlighting so that you can see these results:

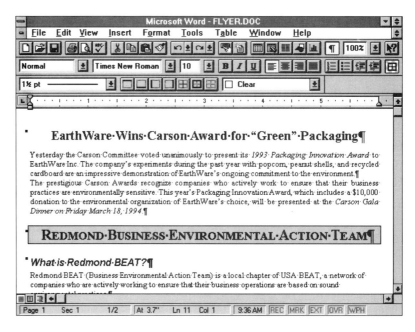

6. Again, you might want to experiment with the other possible border and shading options. Then click the Borders button on the Formatting toolbar to turn off the Borders toolbar.

Turning off the Borders toolbar

Setting Up Multiple Columns

Newsletters and flyers often feature multicolumn layouts like those of magazines and newspapers. These layouts give you more flexibility when it comes to the placement of elements on the page, and they are often visually more interesting than single-column layouts. We already introduced you to columns in Chapter 3, when you worked with Word's newsletter template. But what if you want to use multiple columns in a document based on a different template? With Word, setting up multiple columns for an entire document couldn't be easier. You click the Columns button on the toolbar and select the number of columns you want. When you want only part of your document to have a multicolumn layout, you select that part of the document before clicking the Columns button.

Creating columns

However, sometimes things aren't quite so simple. Word puts a default amount of space between columns, but suppose we don't want to use the default spacing. To create a three-column layout with 0.25 inch of space between columns, follow these steps:

1. Select the text from *What is Redmond BEAT?* to the period following the telephone number in the last sentence.

2. Choose Columns from the Format menu to display the dialog box shown here:

Creating a three-column layout

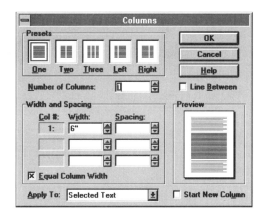

3. Click Three in the Presets section. Next, in the Width And Spacing section, change the entry in column 1's Spacing edit box to *0.25*.

4. Check that Selected Text is selected as the Apply To option, and click OK. Word puts a section break (a double dotted line with *End of Section* at its center) at the beginning of the selected text and another at the end, and reformats the text so that it snakes across the page in three columns. However, because you are in normal view, you see only one skinny column on the left side of your screen.

5. Click anywhere to remove the highlight, and then click the Print Preview button on the toolbar to see the effects of the three-column layout.

6. Now let's look at the document in page layout view, a cross between print preview and normal view that allows you to see the layout of your document at a size that allows efficient editing and formatting. Click the Page Layout View button at the left end of the horizontal scroll bar, and then scroll until the *REDMOND BUSINESS ENVIRONMENTAL ACTION*

Document sections

When applying different formatting, such as different numbers of columns or different margins, to only part of a document, Word designates the beginning and end of that part with section breaks. You can insert section breaks manually by choosing Break from the Insert menu, selecting an option in the Section Breaks section, and then clicking OK. You can have the new section start at the top of the next new page, at the top of the next even page, or at the top of the next odd page; or you can have the new section continue immediately after the old section.

TEAM title is at the top of the window, which now looks like the one below:

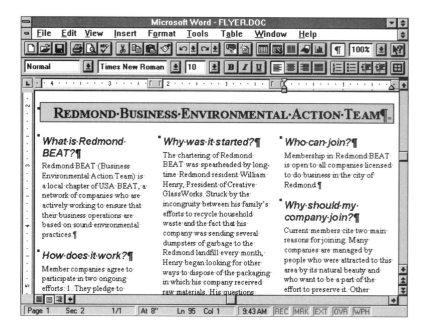

Creating Lists

The second paragraph of the backgrounder contains two numbered items that would stand out better if they were set up in a list format. Word has two built-in list formats: one for numbered lists and one for bulleted lists. Here's how you implement the numbered list format (the bulleted list format works the same way):

1. Click an insertion point to the left of the number 1 in the second paragraph, and then press Enter.

2. Next click an insertion point to the left of the number 2, and press Enter. The numbered items now appear in their own paragraphs.

3. Select the new paragraphs, and click the Numbering button on the Formatting toolbar. Then remove the highlight to see these results:

Bulleted lists

To create a bulleted list, you select the paragraphs you want to be bulleted and click the Bullets button on the Formatting toolbar. By default, Word precedes each paragraph with a large, round dot. You can change the bullet symbol by choosing Bullets And Numbering from the Format menu and selecting one of five other standard symbols. You can modify the format of bulleted paragraphs the same way you modify numbered paragraphs (see the facing page).

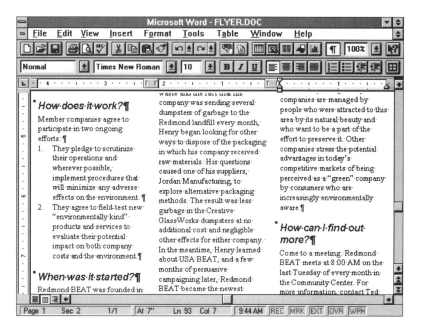

Word has given the two paragraphs a hanging-indent format. (If they were not already numbered, Word would have numbered them too.)

The space between the numbers and their text is a little too wide for the skinny column, so let's adjust the indent of the numbered list:

1. Select the two numbered items, and choose Bullets And Numbering from the Format menu to display this dialog box:

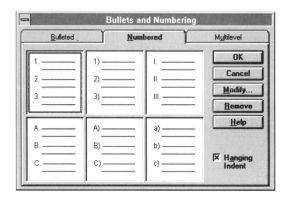

2. Select the Numbered tab, if it isn't already selected, and then click the Modify button to display the dialog box shown on the next page.

Using special symbols

You can use a different symbol for the bullet in bulleted lists by choosing Bullets And Numbering from the Format menu, clicking the Modify button, and then clicking Bullet to display the Symbol dialog box. Select the font and symbol you want, and click OK twice to return to your document with the new symbol in place. The next time you click the Bullets button, Word will use the new symbol when creating a bulleted item. To insert a special symbol elsewhere in a document, simply choose Symbol from the Insert menu, select the font and symbol you want, and click Insert.

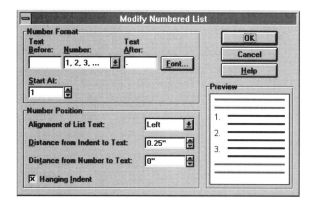

3. Change the setting in the Distance From Indent To Text edit box to *0.15*, and click OK. Word closes up the space.

Adding Headers and Footers

The flyer is currently only one page long. For documents that are longer than one page, you'll probably want to add a header or footer, so we'll show you how to do that next.

Headers are printed in the top margin of the page, and footers are printed in the bottom margin. They usually carry such repeating information as page numbers, dates, and company names. They're invaluable for long documents, such as reports, but can be used to add a professional touch to documents of any length. With Word, you have many header and footer options. For example, you can create:

Header and footer options

• Identical headers and footers for every page.

• A different header and footer for the first page.

• Different headers and footers for left (even) pages and right (odd) pages.

• Different headers and footers for each section of a document.

For this example, we'll create a header that appears on all pages except the first and a footer that prints on all pages. To create a header on all but the first page of a document, you tell Word that you want the first page to have a different header from the remaining pages, and then you leave the first page header blank. To create this type of header, we need to add at least one more page to the flyer, like this:

1. Press Ctrl+End to move to the end of the document, and then choose Break from the Insert menu to display this dialog box:

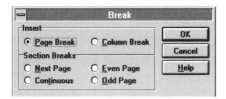

Inserting a page break

2. Accept the default Page Break option by clicking OK.

3. Then insert another page break using a different method: Press Ctrl+Enter. Your document now has three pages.

4. Press Ctrl+Home to move to the top of the document.

Now let's tackle the header and footer:

1. Choose Header And Footer from the View menu. Word dims the text of the document, outlines the space in which the header will appear with a dotted box, and displays this Header And Footer floating toolbar:

The Header And Footer toolbar

Odd and even

You can create different headers and footers for odd and even pages by selecting the Different Odd And Even option on the Layout tab of the Page Setup dialog box. Word then indicates whether you are creating an odd or even header or footer in the box at the top or bottom of your document. The headers and footers you create using this option are automatically reflected on all odd and even pages of the document. For example, you might use this technique to create headers similar to those at the top of the pages of this book.

2. Click the Page Setup button on the Header And Footer toolbar to display this dialog box:

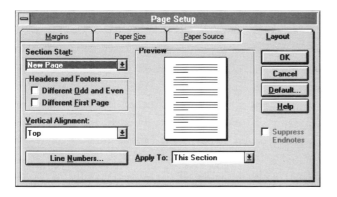

If necessary, click the Layout tab to display its options.

1. In the Headers And Footers section, select the Different First Page option, and click OK. Word changes the header designation to read *First Page Header - Section 1*.

Switching between headers and footers

2. We're going to leave the first page header blank, so click the Switch Between Header And Footer button on the Header And Footer toolbar to jump to the bottom of the page.

You can type any text you want in a header or footer, and you can then format the text in the same way you would format document text. With the buttons on the Header And Footer toolbar, you can tell Word to insert page number, date, and time fields. Word then replaces the page number field with the correct page number for each page, and replaces the date and time fields with the current date and time from your computer's system clock.

For the sample footer, let's put some text and the date on the left and page numbers on the right:

1. Type *Revised* and a space, click the Date button, type a space, and then type *by Ted Lee*.

2. Next press Tab twice, type *Page* and a space, and click the Page Numbers button. The footer now looks like this:

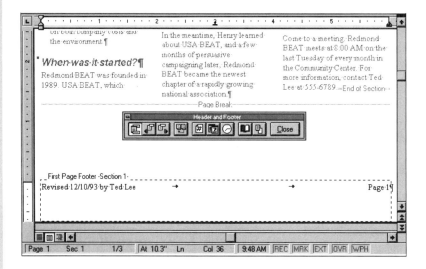

Now let's format the footer so that it stands out on the page. We'll leave the font and size as they are, but we'll make the footer bold and we'll add a line above it:

More about page numbers

If you want your headers or footers to contain nothing but page numbers, you don't have to create a header or footer. You can have Word perform this chore for you. Choose Page Numbers from the Insert menu, and in the Page Numbers dialog box, specify whether the page numbers should appear at the top or bottom of the page, how they should be aligned, and whether a number should appear on the first page, and click OK. Whether you add page numbers this way or by clicking the Page Numbers button on the Header And Footer toolbar, you can format them by clicking the Format button in the Page Numbers dialog box. You can select from five numbering schemes, including Arabic numbers (1, 2, 3), lower-/uppercase letters (a, b, c/A, B, C), and lower-/uppercase Roman numerals (i, ii, iii/I, II, III); specify whether chapter numbers should be included; and select a starting number.

1. Select the footer by clicking once in the selection bar adjacent to the footer, and then click the Bold button.

Formatting the footer

2. Click the Borders button on the Formatting toolbar to turn on the Borders toolbar, and then click the Top Border button to draw a line above the footer.

Adding a separator line

3. Click anywhere in the footer to remove the highlight and see the results:

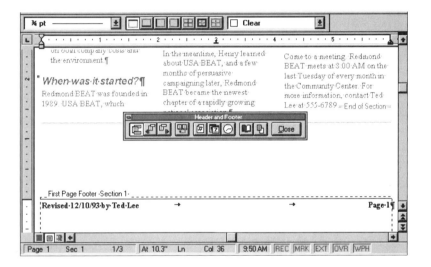
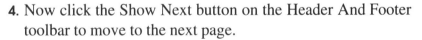
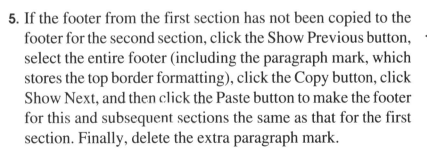

4. Now click the Show Next button on the Header And Footer toolbar to move to the next page.

5. If the footer from the first section has not been copied to the footer for the second section, click the Show Previous button, select the entire footer (including the paragraph mark, which stores the top border formatting), click the Copy button, click Show Next, and then click the Paste button to make the footer for this and subsequent sections the same as that for the first section. Finally, delete the extra paragraph mark.

Next let's tackle the header:

1. Click the Switch Between Header And Footer button to move up to the header at the top of the second page. Then click the Same As Previous button to toggle it off, thereby indicating that you want this header to be different from the first one.

2. Now type *Redmond Business Environmental Action Team*, and make it bold, centered, and small caps (see page 88). Then follow the steps on page 89 to add a border and shading so that the header looks like this:

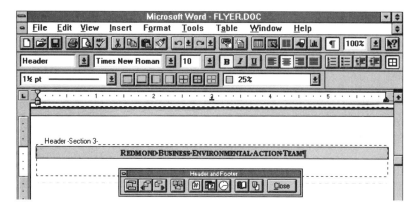

3. Click the Close button to return to page layout view, and click the Borders button to turn off the Borders toolbar.

Let's take a quick look at the document in print preview:

Viewing multiple pages

1. Click the Print Preview button. Then click the Multiple Pages button on the Print Preview toolbar to drop down a grid of "pages," and drag through the left and center "pages" in the top row. Word displays the first two pages of your document side by side, like this:

Line numbers

To number the lines in a document, choose Page Setup from the File menu, and on the Layout tab, click the Line Numbers button. In the Line Numbers dialog box, click the Add Line Numbering check box, indicate the starting line number and the increment (the default for both settings is 1), and where numbering should be restarted (for example, with each new page). Then click OK twice to add the line numbers, which can be viewed in page layout view or print preview.

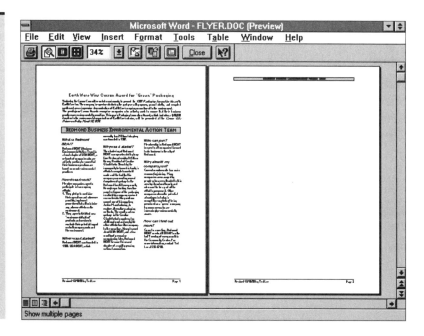

2. Press PageDown to see the third page, and then click the Close button on the Print Preview toolbar.

3. Before going any further, remove one of the page breaks by pressing Ctrl+End to move to the end of the document and then pressing Backspace. (We'll use the second page in the next chapter.)

Adding Footnotes

Footnotes are used to document sources and give tangential tidbits of information when their inclusion in the main text would detract from the discussion. We are including a brief overview of footnotes in this chapter because they involve a special kind of formatting. Their reference marks in the text are usually superscripted, and the footnotes themselves are usually gathered at the bottom of the page or at the end of the document. Fortunately, Word takes care of a lot of the necessary formatting for you.

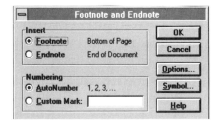

As an example, suppose you want to mention the origin of the Carson Committee in the flyer, but you can't think of a graceful way of including it in the press release. The simple solution is to put the information in a footnote. Here's how:

1. Press Ctrl+Home to move to the top of the document, and then click an insertion point after the word *Committee* in the first paragraph of the press release.

2. Choose Footnote from the Insert menu to display the dialog box shown here:

By default, Word automatically numbers footnotes and places them at the bottom of the page.

Footnote basics

Footnote placement

By default, Word places footnotes at the bottom of the page. You can have Word place them after the last line of text on a page. (This last option is useful for pages that are less than full length.) You can also place them at the end of a section or the end of the document, in which case they are called endnotes. Click Options in the Footnote And Endnote dialog box to change the default placement.

3. Click OK. Word inserts a superscripted 1 after the word *Committee* and moves to the bottom of the page, ready for you to type the footnote.

Typing the footnote in place

4. Type the following, formatting *The Silent Spring* in italics:

Author of The Silent Spring, *an apocryphal vision of the results of people's thoughtless manipulation of the environment for their own short-term needs, Rachel Carson was a revered pioneer environmentalist.*

Your screen looks like this:

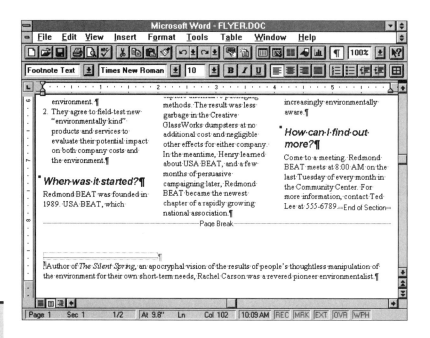

Footnote and endnote options

Clicking Options in the Footnote And Endnote dialog box accesses the Note Options dialog box. In addition to specifying footnote or endnote placement, you can change the number format, start footnote or endnote numbering at a number other than 1, and specify that numbering is to restart with each new section or page.

5. Click the down arrow to the right of the Zoom Control button on the toolbar, and select Whole Page from the list of options so that you can see exactly how Word will position the footnote when you print the document. Then select 100% from the Zoom Control list to return to regular page layout view.

That's the simple way to create footnotes. You can also assign your own reference marks to footnotes. But why complicate things? Our advice is to let Word keep track of footnotes with automatically numbered reference marks so that you can concentrate on more important matters.

Formatting with Styles

You can work through a document applying formats to headings and other special paragraphs one by one, but Word provides an easier way: You can store custom combinations of formatting by defining the combination as a *style*. You can then apply that combination to a text selection or a paragraph simply by selecting the style from the Style drop-down list on the Formatting toolbar. Just as there are two types of formatting—character formatting and paragraph formatting—there are two types of styles—character styles and paragraph styles. In this chapter, we focus primarily on paragraph styles because people tend to use them more frequently.

Although you may not have realized it, every paragraph you write has a style. When you create a new document based on the Normal template, Word applies the Normal style to all paragraphs unless instructed otherwise. The Normal style formats characters as 10-point regular Times New Roman and paragraphs as single-spaced and left-aligned. For example, the paragraphs of the letter you wrote in Chapter 1 all had the Normal style. The paragraphs of the backgrounder you created in Chapter 2 all started out with the Normal style, but when you assigned first and second levels to the headings (see page 46), Word responded by applying the Heading 1 and Heading 2 styles to those paragraphs. When you base a document on a template other than Normal, the styles included as part of that template become available, and as you saw in Chapter 3, you can then create documents like the press release simply by filling in the paragraphs of the template.

Because the flyer consists of the press release and backgrounder files, the styles saved as part of those documents have been carried over into FLYER.DOC. Try this:

1. Click the Normal View button at the left end of the horizontal scroll bar, scroll up to the shaded backgrounder title (if necessary), and click an insertion point in it. Notice that the Style box on the formatting toolbar shows that the Heading 1 style is applied to this paragraph.

Style basics

The Normal style

Character styles vs. paragraph styles

Character styles affect only the selected text and apply their formats on top of any paragraph formats applied to the selected text. Paragraph styles affect the entire paragraph containing the insertion point. For example, you can apply a paragraph style that makes an entire paragraph 12-point regular Arial and then select the first word and apply a character style that makes just that word 18-point bold italic Arial.

2. Now press the Down Arrow key several times, noting how the Style box changes to reflect the style of the paragraph that contains the insertion point.

Displaying the style area

3. Choose Options from the bottom of the Tools menu, click the View tab if the View options are not already displayed, and enter *0.6* in the Style Area Width edit box in the bottom-left corner. Click OK. Your screen then looks something like the one shown here:

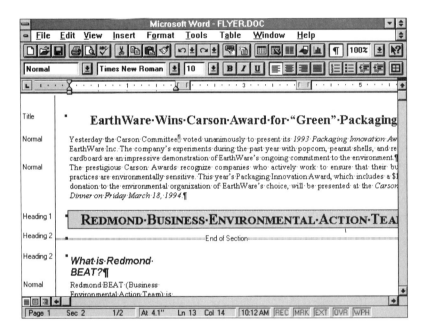

As you can see, Word has opened a style area along the left edge of the screen, pushing your text to the right. The style applied to each paragraph appears in the style area. This view of your document allows you to see at a glance which styles are controlling the formatting of this document.

Closing the style area

4. Point to the line to the right of the style area, and when the pointer changes to a vertical bar with two opposing arrows, drag the line all the way to the left edge of your screen to close the style area.

Using Word's Predefined Styles

As you know, Word comes with nine predefined heading styles, one for each of the heading levels you can designate when using the Outlining feature. Word also has predefined paragraph styles for a number of other common document elements, such as index entries, headers and footers, and footnotes. However, if you create a new document by clicking the New button on the toolbar and immediately pull down the Style list by clicking the arrow to the right of the Style box, you'll see that the list of available styles includes only Default Paragraph Font, Heading 1, Heading 2, Heading 3, and Normal. Default Paragraph Font appears in regular type to indicate that it is a character style, and the other four styles appear in bold type to indicate that they are paragraph styles. Word does not list the other predefined styles unless the current document contains the corresponding elements. If you insert one of these elements in the document, Word both applies the style to the element and adds the style name to the Style list. Check this out:

Available styles for new documents

1. Click the down arrow to the right of the Style box to drop down the Style list.

2. Scroll through the list. You'll see that Word has added the styles from the press release template, as well as styles for the footnote reference, footnote text, footers, and headers you inserted earlier in the chapter.

3. Press Esc to close the list without making any changes.

When Word applies one of its built-in styles to an element, it uses the formatting that has been predefined for that element. Once the style is available on the Style list, you can apply the style to other paragraphs. You can also redefine the style to suit the document you are creating. We tell you how to apply and modify styles on page 106.

Creating Custom Styles

Although Word does a good job of anticipating the document elements for which you will need styles, you will undoubtedly want to come up with styles of your own. You create custom styles by formatting a paragraph the way you want it and then defining that combination of formats as a style. After a style is defined, you can modify it and use it as the basis for creating new styles.

Defining Styles

The paragraphs of the press release currently have no space between them and no first-line indent, making it hard to tell at a glance where one paragraph ends and another begins. To demonstrate the process of defining a style, let's create a style that indents the first line of each paragraph and makes the size of the characters slightly larger:

1. Move to the top of the document, and then right-click any-where in the first text paragraph to display the paragraph's shortcut menu.

2. Choose Paragraph from the shortcut menu to display this dialog box:

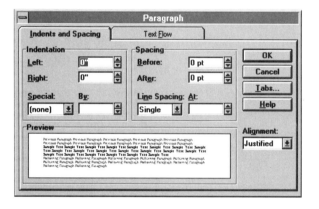

Creating a first-line indent →
3. In the Indentation section, select First Line from the Special drop-down list. Word enters *0.5"* in the By edit box as the default first-line indent, and shows in the Preview box below how your text will look with this setting.

4. Pause for a moment to notice the effect of this new setting, and then click OK to return to the flyer.

5. The paragraphs would look more balanced if the indent aligned with the heading above, so choose Paragraph from the Format menu, change the setting in the By edit box to *0.35*, and click OK.

6. Now select the entire paragraph, and then select 12 from the Font Size box on the Formatting toolbar. Here are the results:

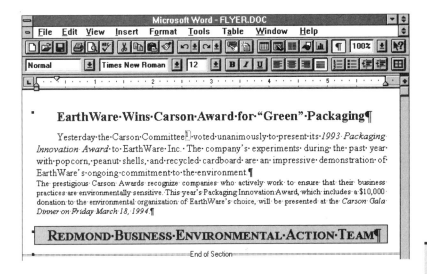

Next, you need to define this particular combination of formatting as a style. Here goes:

1. With the insertion point located in the first paragraph of the press release, click Normal in the Style box to highlight it.

2. Type *Para Indent* (for *indented paragraph*), the name you want to assign to this style. Then press Enter. Word creates the style, adds the style name to the Style list, and displays Para Indent in the Style box to indicate that it is the style applied to the current paragraph.

Now let's turn our attention to the backgrounder part of the flyer. Suppose you want to justify these paragraphs and add a little space before each one. (Paragraphs with space before them are called *open paragraphs*.) Follow these steps:

1. Right-click the first text paragraph of the backgrounder, and choose the Paragraph command from the shortcut menu.

2. Drop down the Alignment list in the bottom-right corner of the Paragraph dialog box, and select Justified. (This is the equivalent of clicking the Justify button on the Formatting toolbar.)

3. In the Spacing section, change the Before setting to *3 pt*, and click OK.

4. Now click Normal in the Style box to highlight it, type *Para Open* as this style's name, and then press Enter.

AutoFormat

Word's AutoFormat feature analyzes all or part of a document and automatically assigns styles to its paragraphs based on how they are used and how they relate to other paragraphs. Word doesn't always reach the right conclusions after analyzing a document, but it usually gives you a good starting point for further formatting. To automatically format a document, click the AutoFormat button on the toolbar. (To format only part of a document, select that part before clicking AutoFormat.) You can use the Undo button to reverse the formatting if it completely misses the mark. Or you can choose AutoFormat from the Format menu to have the option of accepting all the formatting; rejecting all the formatting; or reviewing and accepting/rejecting each format in turn. You can also select a custom style from the Style Gallery (see the tip on page 114) or set AutoFormat options, including which paragraphs Word will apply styles to and how quotation marks and symbols will be treated.

That's it! You now have two custom styles available on the Style list. Defining styles is that easy. Let's look at how you modify styles—an equally simple process.

Modifying Styles

Suppose you want to globally change the formatting produced by the Heading 2 style. Try this:

1. Select the entire *What Is Redmond BEAT?* heading. Click the Center button on the Formatting toolbar, and then select 10 from the Font Size list.

Redefining an existing style

2. Now redefine the style based on the new formatting combination by dropping down the Style list and selecting Heading 2. Word displays this dialog box:

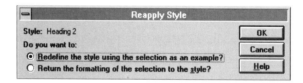

If you select Redefine, Word modifies the existing style. If you select Return, Word applies the selected style to the paragraph, returning the paragraph to its condition before you made changes to the formatting. Clicking Cancel closes the dialog box, leaving your formatting changes intact without redefining the style.

3. You want to redefine the style, so click OK.

4. Now scroll down through the backgrounder text, noticing that every second-level heading has instantly changed to 10 points with center alignment.

As you have seen, you can also modify a style and then store the new formatting combination with a different name so that the original style is preserved.

Applying Styles

So far, the Para Indent style is applied only to the paragraph you used when creating the style. Let's apply this style to the next paragraph:

1. Click an insertion point in the second paragraph of the press release, drop down the Style list, and select the Para Indent style. Word changes the paragraph from Normal style to Para Indent style, and your document now looks like this:

Applying styles from
the Style list

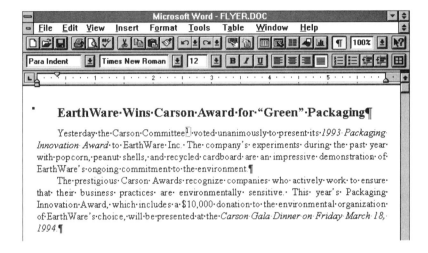

If the press release included more than two paragraphs, you could apply the style to the remaining paragraphs by selecting text from all the paragraphs and then applying the style.

Applying styles to
multiple paragraphs

Now try a different procedure to apply the Para Open style to the paragraphs of the backgrounder:

1. First click in the second text paragraph of the backgrounder (which has the Normal style), and apply the Para Open style from the Style list.

2. Then click in the next text paragraph (the first numbered item), and press Ctrl+Y to repeat the previous command. Don't worry that the new style messes up the numbered-list formatting. We'll take care of that in a moment.

Applying styles from
the keyboard

3. Repeat step 2 for all remaining text paragraphs.

4. Now go back and select the second and third paragraphs under the *How does it work?* heading, and click the Numbering button on the Formatting toolbar. Because you are applying the numbered-list format "on top of" the Para Open style, the numbered items are now justified and have 3 points of space above them, just like all the other paragraphs. The results are shown on the next page.

Applying a format
"on top of" a style

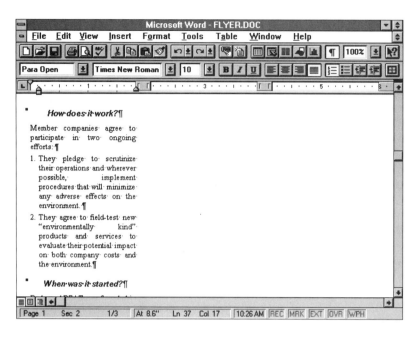

Notice that Word has retained the 0.15" setting that you specified earlier for the numbered-list indent.

Applying Styles as You Type

Generally, paragraphs "inherit" the style of the paragraph from which they are created. Let's see how this works:

1. Open up the style area by choosing Options from the Tools menu, setting the Style Area Width option on the View tab to *0.6*, and clicking OK.

2. Click an insertion point at the end of the second press release paragraph, and press Enter to insert a new paragraph. Notice that the new paragraph has the same Para Indent style as the preceding paragraph.

3. Select the Heading 2 style from the Style list. Word changes the designation in the style area to Heading 2. Now type a few characters. Word formats the characters with the Heading 2 style as you type them.

If styles occur in a particular sequence in a document, you can override the style inheritance rule. For example, if headings are always followed by regular paragraphs, you can specify that pressing Enter at the end of a Heading 2 paragraph will initiate a Normal paragraph instead of another Heading 2

Style shortcuts

To apply a style from the keyboard, press Ctrl+Shift+S, type the name of the style, and press Enter. If the Formatting toolbar is hidden, pressing Ctrl+Shift+S displays the Style dialog box, where you can double-click the desired style. You can apply some styles directly from the keyboard. For the Heading 1 style, press Alt+Ctrl+1; for the Heading 2 style, press Alt+Ctrl+2; and for the Heading 3 style, press Alt+Ctrl+3. To apply the List Bullet style, press Ctrl+Shift+L. To return a paragraph to the Normal style, press Ctrl+Shift+N or Alt+Shift+5 on the numeric keypad.

paragraph. Word has already set up this sequence for its predefined heading styles. Try this:

1. Press Enter at the end of the second-level heading you just created. Notice that the new paragraph has the Normal style, not the Heading 2 style. Let's see how this relationship is established.

2. Without moving the insertion point, choose Style from the Format menu to display this dialog box:

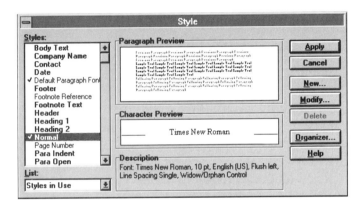

3. Click the Modify button to display the dialog box shown here:

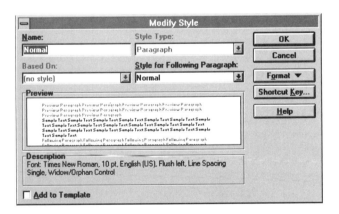

The Style For Following Paragraph box specifies the style that will be applied to the next paragraph you create. As you can see, the next paragraph you create by pressing Enter will inherit the Normal style of the current paragraph.

4. Click Cancel to close the Modify Style dialog box.

Finding and replacing styles

To search for paragraphs to which you have assigned a particular style, choose Find from the Edit menu, click the Format button, and then click Style. In the Find Style dialog box, select the style you want to find, click OK to return to the Find dialog box, and click Find Next. Word highlights the next paragraph formatted with that style. You can use the Edit menu's Replace command to change a particular applied style. For example, to change the Para Indent style to the Para Open style, choose Replace from the Edit menu, click Format and then Style, select Para Indent, and click OK. Then click the Replace With edit box, click Format and then Style, select Para Open, and click OK. With the Find What and Replace With edit boxes set up, click either Find Next and then Replace or Replace All, depending on whether you want Word to pause so that you can confirm the replacement of the specified style.

5. In the Style dialog box, click Heading 2 in the Styles list, and click Modify again. The Style For Following Paragraph edit box specifies that the next paragraph you create by pressing Enter will not inherit the Heading 2 style but will instead have the Normal style.

6. Click Cancel twice to close the dialog boxes. Then delete the demonstration heading and blank paragraph, and close the style area by resetting Style Area Width in the Options dialog box to *0* or by dragging the style area border to the left.

Transferring Styles to Other Documents

Once you have created a style for use in one document, you don't have to recreate it for use in others. You can simply copy the style to the new document. Or if you want the style to become a part of the set of styles available with a particular template, you can copy the style to that template. Try this:

1. Click the New button on the toolbar to create a new blank document based on the Normal template.

2. Drop down the Style list, which shows the Default Paragraph Font, Heading 1, Heading 2, Heading 3, and Normal styles that are predefined for the Normal template.

3. Close the blank document.

The Style command

You can create and modify styles without selecting existing text by choosing the Style command from the Format menu. The Style dialog box lists the styles that have been defined for the current document. You can select a style to see its description and how sample text looks with that style applied. You can click the New button to define a new style and the Modify button to modify a style you have selected from the list. Clicking Delete removes the selected style.

4. Now with FLYER.DOC on your screen, choose Style from the Format menu, and in the Style dialog box, click the Organizer button to display this dialog box:

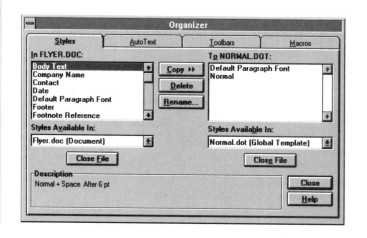

As you can see, the styles available in FLYER.DOC are listed on the left, and two of the styles available in the Normal template (which is stored as a file called NORMAL.DOT) are listed on the right.

5. Next scroll the FLYER.DOC list, and select Para Indent. The style's formatting description appears in the Description box at the bottom of the dialog box.

6. Click the Copy button. Word copies the Para Indent style to NORMAL.DOT.

7. Repeat steps 5 and 6 for the Para Open style, and then click the Close button (not the Close File button).

8. Click the New button to open a blank document based on the Normal template, and then drop down the Style list, which now contains Para Indent and Para Open in addition to the predefined styles.

9. Close the new document without saving it.

This discussion of styles has been necessarily brief, but you now know enough to begin using styles effectively. The most important advice we can give you regarding styles is: Use them. Within a few hours, they will be second nature, and you will wonder how you ever got along without them.

As you probably realize, we are not quite finished with the flyer. The basic formatting is in place, but it needs one or two little touches to make it look more professional. First we'll hyphenate the text to close up some of the spacey lines. Then we'll check the balance of the flyer on the page and, if necessary, we'll adjust the margins.

Hyphenating Documents

By default, Word does not hyphenate your text, but by hyphenating some words you can really improve the looks of the justified skinny columns of the backgrounder. Follow the steps on the next page.

The Organizer

You use the Organizer to help organize the elements available with specific documents and templates. The Organizer dialog box enables you not only to copy, delete, and rename styles, but also AutoText entries, toolbars, and macros. By using the Organizer, you can ensure that all your documents and templates contain only the elements they need.

1. Press Ctrl+Home to move to the top of the document. (You may as well hyphenate the press release text, too.) Then choose Hyphenation from the Tools menu to display this dialog box:

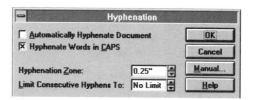

Automatic hyphenation

2. Select the Automatically Hyphenate Document option, and click the Hyphenate Words In CAPS option to deselect it (you don't want to hyphenate BEAT, for example). Then click OK. Word quickly hyphenates the document.

3. Scroll through the flyer, noticing the effects of hyphenation. Many of the big spaces between words have disappeared, and the flyer now looks much more attractive. (You can make the last line of the backgrounder less spacey by clicking an insertion point after the period following the telephone number and pressing Enter.)

Adjusting Margins

Only after you have made all your other formatting adjustments should you turn your attention to the margin settings. Why? Because little changes can have big consequences in the formatting world. Take hyphenation, for example. It's not uncommon for a document to end up a couple of lines shorter after you use the Hyphenation command, and a couple of lines can make a big difference, especially when it comes to balancing the text in columns. With that said, let's see how to adjust the margins. Start by checking the balance of the document:

Checking page balance

1. Press Ctrl+Home to move to the top of the document, and then click the Page Layout View button at the left end of the horizontal scroll bar.

2. Select Two Pages from the Zoom Control list on the toolbar. Your screen looks like this:

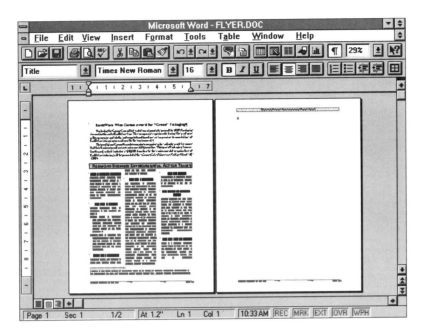

As you can see, we need to adjust the margins so that the text starts a little higher on the first page. Follow these steps:

1. Choose Page Setup from the File menu to display this dialog box (if necessary, click the Margins tab):

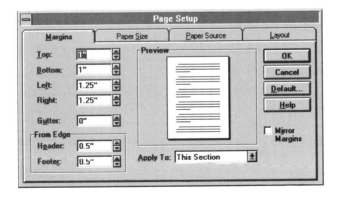

You can also double-click a ruler in page layout view or print preview to display the Page Setup dialog box, the settings in which control the basic layout of the document's pages.

2. Change the setting in the Top edit box to *0.5*, check that the Apply To option is This Section (you don't want any text you add to the second page to run into the header, which sits 0.5 inch from the top of the page), and click OK. Word adjusts the text to fit the new margin.

Fitting everything on one page

If your document is longer than one page but you want to print it on only one page, you can display the document in print preview and then adjust the top, bottom, left, and right margins using the horizontal and vertical rulers. As a last resort, you can click the Shrink To Fit button on the Print Preview toolbar. Word then adjusts the font size to try and make everything fit.

3. Select 100% from the Zoom Control list, and insert a column break at the beginning of the *Why was it started?* and *Who can join?* headings (see page 83).

4. Select Whole Page from the Zoom Control list to see these results:

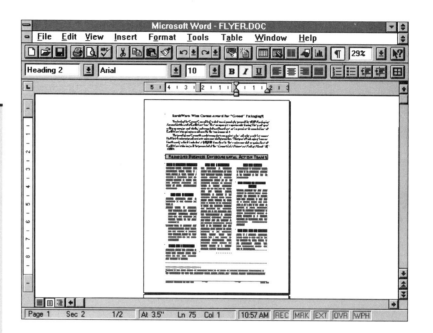

Attaching a different template to a document

To attach a different template to a document, choose Templates from the File menu, type the name of the template you want in the Document Template edit box, and click OK. (If you want to include the template's styles in the Style list, be sure to select the Automatically Update Document Styles option.) If you can't remember the name of the template, click the Attach button, locate the template you want in the Attach Template dialog box, and click OK twice. If you don't know which template you want, choose Style Gallery from the Format menu. The Style Gallery dialog box lists the available templates and allows you to preview what the current document will look like with a selected template attached. You can also view samples of the styles available in the selected template and a sample document formatted with those styles.

5. Save the finished document, and then print it. Your flyer should look like the one at the beginning of the chapter.

Creating Custom Templates

As you use Word for Windows in your daily work, you will probably find yourself creating the same kinds of documents over and over again. Memos, letters, newsletters—every day, every week, every month. What you create and how often will depend on your job. But regardless, you won't want to start from scratch every time. Sometimes you'll be able to use Word's predefined templates for these standard documents; other times, you'll want to create your own templates.

You can save any document as a template, and then open a new document based on that template every time you need to create that type of document. The new document faithfully reflects the margins and formatting of the original and even makes available any styles, dictionaries, and AutoText entries you have assigned to the template. (We discussed styles on page 101, dictionaries on page 55, and AutoText on page 35.) All you have to do is type the text and make any special adjustments necessary for the document you're working on. Word takes care of everything else for you.

Obviously, before all this magic can happen, you have to create the template, and that's what this section is all about. Since we've already done all the formatting, let's create a FLYER template as an example. Follow these steps:

1. Choose Save As from the File menu.

2. Click the down arrow to the right of the Save File As Type edit box, and select Document Template. Word displays the list of files stored in the WINWORD\TEMPLATE directory.

3. Click OK to save the template with the name Word suggests: FLYER.DOT. (As mentioned in Chapter 3, the DOT extension indicates that the file is a template.)

4. Choose Close from the File menu.

That's all there is to it. Next, let's see how you would use the new template:

1. Choose New from the File menu. Word displays the New dialog box.

2. Leave Document selected in the New section, and double-click Flyer in the Template list. Word opens a new document that looks just like your template, except that Document$X$ is in the title bar, indicating that you have not yet assigned the document a name.

You can now replace the text of the flyer to create the new document and then save it with a new name.

Saving documents in other formats

To save a document in a format other than that of a normal Word document, follow the steps for saving a template, selecting the format you want from the Save File As Type list. For example, to save a document in ASCII (text-only) format so that it can be opened by other applications, choose Save As from the File menu, name the document, select Text Only from the Save File As Type list, and click OK. (ASCII means *American Standard Code for Information Interchange.*)

Graphic Impact: Graphics, Tables, Charts, and Spreadsheets

What you will learn...

Import graphics for illustrations and decoration

EarthWare Wins Carson Award for "Green" Packaging

Yesterday the Carson Committee[1] voted unanimously to present its *1993 Packaging Innovation Award* to EarthWare Inc. The company's experiments during the past year with popcorn, peanut shells, and recycled cardboard are an impressive demonstration of EarthWare's ongoing commitment to the environment.

The prestigious Carson Awards recognize companies who actively work to ensure that their business practices are environmentally sensitive. This year's Packaging Innovation Award, which includes a $10,000 donation to the environmental organization of EarthWare's choice, will be presented at the *Carson Gala Dinner on Friday March 18, 1994.*

REDMOND BU

What is Redmond BEA

Redmond BEAT (Business
vironmental Action Team)
local chapter of USA BEA
network of companies who
actively working to ensure
their business operations
based on sound environme
practices.

How does it work?

Member companies agree
participate in two ongoing
forts:

1. They pledge to scruti
   their operations and wher
   possible, implement pr
   dures that will minimize
   adverse effects on the e
   ronment.

2. They agree to field-test
   "environmentally kind" p
   ucts and services to eval
   their potential impact on
   company costs and the e
   ronment.

When was it started?

Redmond BEAT was founde
1989. USA BEAT, which
rently has 210 local chap
was founded in 1987.

---

[1] Author of *The Silent Spring*
the environment for their ow

Revised 12/10/93 by Ted Le

Create and format tables visually—no need to set tabs

Perform calculations with formulas

Present your data visually with Graph

Import a spreadsheet as a Word table

AIR POLLUTANT SOURCES In Millions of Metric Tons			
Contributor	Carbon Monoxide	Sulfur Dioxide	Nitrogen Oxides
Transportation	41.2	0.9	8.1
Industrial Emissions	4.7	3.4	0.6
Fuel Combustion	7.6	16.4	10.8
Solid-Waste Burning	1.7	--	0.1
Miscellaneous	6.0	--	0.2
TOTAL	61.2	20.7	19.8
AVERAGE	12.24	6.9	3.96

AIR POLLUTANT SOURCES
In Millions of Metric Tons

(bar chart: Nitrogen Oxides, Sulfur Dioxide, Carbon Monoxide for categories Miscellaneous, Solid-Waste Burning, Fuel Combustion, Industrial Emissions, Transportation; x-axis 0 10 20 30 40 50)

MUNICIPAL WASTE			
Class	**Type**	**Millions of Tons**	**% of Total**
Paper	Newspaper	8.8	6.25
	Commercial Printing	3.2	2.27
	Books and Magazines	4.4	3.13
	Office Paper	5	3.55
	Other Paper (Non-Packaging)	8.3	5.9
	Containers and Packaging (Paper)	20.4	14.5
Total		**50.1**	**35.61**
Other	Containers and Packaging (Non-Paper)	22.3	15.85
	Yard Wastes	28.3	20.11
	Durable Goods	19.1	13.57
	Food Wastes	12.5	8.88
	Miscellaneous	8.4	5.97
Total		**90.6**	**64.38**
GRAND TOTAL		**140.7**	
Source: GARBAGE Magazine, May/June 1990, and Franklin Associates, Ltd.			

While following the examples in the preceding chapters, you've learned a lot about Word's formatting capabilities and how to combine formats to create professional-looking documents. In this chapter, we show you a few tricks for those times when your documents need a little more pizzazz. First we demonstrate how easily you can incorporate graphics into your Word documents. Then we cover how to create tables and charts to present facts and figures. If you've already set up your information in a spreadsheet or database program and don't relish the thought of having to recreate it in Word, you'll be pleased to know that you can import a spreadsheet or database as a Word table.

Importing Word's Graphics

In Chapter 4, you merged the press release you created in Chapter 3 with the backgrounder you created in Chapter 2. The copies were separate text files that, after the merge, became part of the same document. In a similar way, you can merge separate graphics and text files.

Ready-made graphics

The Word for Windows software package includes a number of ready-made graphics files that are suitable for many different types of documents. We'll use one of these files (RECYCLE.WMF) and the flyer from Chapter 4 to demonstrate how easy it is to import graphics in Word. To follow along, you must have the graphics files, which have WMF extensions, installed in the C:\WINWORD\CLIPART directory on your hard disk. If the graphics files haven't been installed, run the Word for Windows setup program to install them.

Supported graphics formats

When you import a graphic created with an application other than Word, Word usually displays the graphic by means of a graphics filter (the exceptions are graphics in WMF and BMP formats, for which no filter is necessary). Word comes with filters for graphics files with the following extensions: CGM, EPS, HGL, PIC, DRW, TIF, WPG, PCX, CDR, and PCT. If the graphics filters were not installed with Word, you can run the Word setup program to install them.

As a demonstration, we'll place the same graphic on either side of the title of the first article in the flyer. If you simply insert a graphic in a document, the document's text will be bumped below the graphic, instead of wrapping beside it. To position the graphic and text side by side, you need to create a frame in which to insert the graphic. With Word for Windows loaded and FLYER.DOC displayed on your screen, follow these steps to create the frame:

1. So that you will be able to see and manipulate the graphic and its frame, start off at the top of the document in page layout

view with Zoom Control set to 100%. If paragraph marks are not visible, click the Show/Hide ¶ button on the toolbar to turn them on.

2. Next choose the Frame command from the Insert menu. The pointer changes to a cross hair.

Creating a frame

3. Position the cross-hair pointer to the left of the word *Earth-Ware* at the beginning of the first article's title. Then hold down the mouse button, and keeping an eye on the ruler, drag to the right about one-half inch and down about one-half inch. (Don't worry about being precise; we'll adjust the frame in a moment.) When you release the mouse button, Word draws a frame the size you indicated, pushing the text to the right to make room, like this:

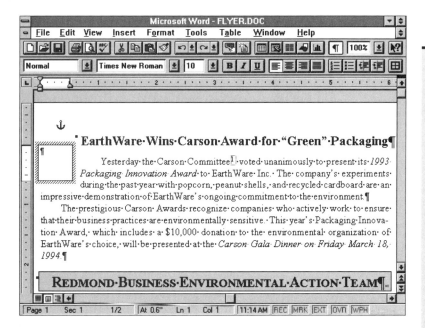

Notice the anchor above the first paragraph, which indicates that the graphic is attached, or anchored, to that paragraph.

4. Save the document with the new name FLYER1.DOC.

Now let's insert a graphic in the frame:

1. Move the pointer over the border surrounding the frame, and when a four-headed arrow appears below the pointer, click to select the frame. Word indicates that the frame is selected by surrounding it with black squares, called *handles*.

Drawing your own graphics

You can create your own simple drawings in Word by using the tools on the Drawing toolbar. Click the Drawing button on the toolbar to switch to page layout view and display the Drawing toolbar across the bottom of your screen. You use the two rightmost buttons to insert a frame and display a drawing window in which you can create your drawing. You use the first five buttons on the left to draw lines, rectangles, ellipses, arcs, and free-form shapes, and the sixth button to create text boxes (see the tip on page 76). You use the Callout button to create labels for your drawings and the Format Callout button to edit and format the labels and leader lines. The remaining buttons manipulate your drawing in various ways—for example, you can change its color and orientation.

Inserting a graphic

2. Choose Picture from the Insert menu to see this dialog box:

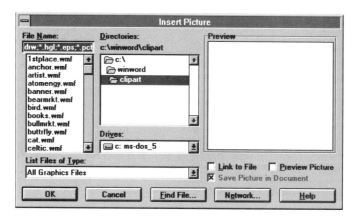

WordArt

Stashed away in the dialog box displayed when you choose Objects from the Insert menu is a great little program called Word-Art. Double-clicking Microsoft WordArt 2.0 in the Object Type list starts this program, which helps you produce striking printed effects with almost any printer. Enter a word or phrase, format it, and then have the program arrange your words in an interesting pattern by selecting from a drop-down palette at the left end of the WordArt toolbar. To quit WordArt, click anywhere outside the WordArt text box. Word then inserts your design as an object in your document. You can then resize it and move it just like any other object. To edit an existing WordArt object, simply double-click it to load both the WordArt program and the object. You can use a WordArt object or combine several objects to produce a logo in a header or to produce text that is larger than the sizes supported by your printer.

3. Scroll the File Name list, select RECYCLE.WMF, and then click Preview Picture to have a look at the picture in the Preview box. Click OK. After a few seconds, Word inserts the graphic in the frame, and this is what you see:

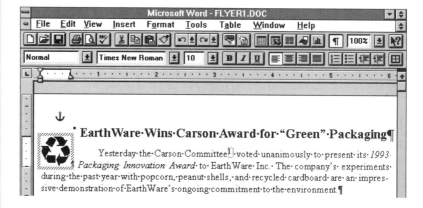

Sizing Graphics

After you import the graphic, you can change its size and shape to suit the needs of your document. For example, you might want to turn the graphic into a small logo, or you might want to enlarge it so that it occupies most of the page. Let's experiment a bit:

1. Select the graphic by clicking it.

2. To increase the graphic's size, position the insertion point on the handle in the bottom-right corner, and when the pointer changes to a two-headed arrow, drag it downward and to the right until the graphic is about 2 inches square.

If you drag the corner handles, you change the size of the graphic without changing the ratio of its width to its height. If you drag the handles in the middle of the sides of the frame, you change this ratio. You can change the width-to-height ratio more precisely by choosing a command. Try this:

1. With the graphic selected, choose Picture from the Format menu. Word displays this dialog box:

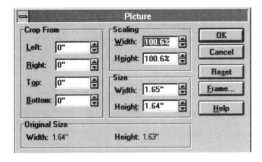

Changing the graphic's scale

2. In the Scaling section, set the Width option to *50%* and the Height option to *100%*, and click OK. Here's the result:

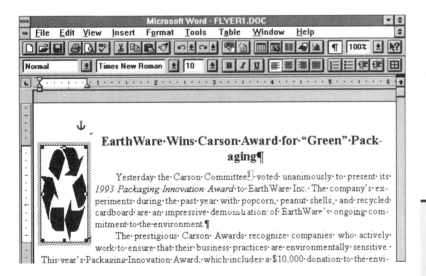

If you want to use only part of the graphic, you can change the size of the frame that contains the graphic without changing the size of the graphic itself. This adjustment has the effect of "cropping" away the parts of the graphic that you don't want to be visible. Follow the steps on the next page.

Editing graphics

To change a graphic, double-click it to load it into a drawing window with the Drawing toolbar displayed. You can then use the buttons on the toolbar to achieve the desired effect. When you are finished, click the drawing window's Close Picture button to return to your document with the updated graphic in place.

Cropping the graphic

1. With the graphic selected, point to the handle in the middle of the bottom of the frame, hold down the Shift key, and drag upward until the frame is about 1 inch square. The pointer changes to the cropping symbol, and the message *Cropping* appears in the status bar. When you release the mouse button, this is what you see:

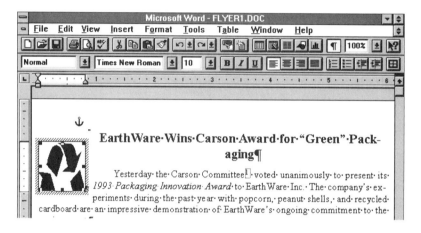

2. Choose Picture from the Format menu. In the Size section of the Picture dialog box, Word has changed the Height setting to reflect the new position of the bottom of the frame.

3. Click Reset to restore the previous settings in the Size and Scaling sections, and then click OK. Word returns the graphic to its original unscaled and uncropped size and proportions.

   After all that experimenting, let's be more precise about the graphic's size and location:

1. Choose Picture from the Format menu, and in the Size section, set the Width and Height to *0.5*. Then click the Frame button to display this dialog box:

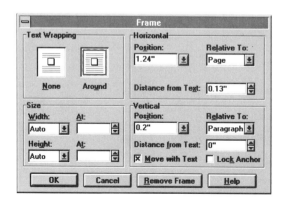

Clicking this button is equivalent to choosing Frame from the Format menu. As you can see, by default Word wraps the text around the frame. If you wanted the text to flow below the frame, you could change this option.

Text wrapping

2. In the Size section, set Width to Exactly and At to *0.5*, and set Height to Exactly and At to *0.5*.

3. In the Horizontal section, set Position to 1.25 and Relative To to Page to put the frame 1.25 inches from the page's left edge.

Positioning the graphic

4. In the Vertical section, set Position to *0.5* and Relative To to Page so that the frame will sit 0.5 inch from the top of the page. Then click OK.

Copying Graphics

For fun, let's copy the graphic and paste it on the other side of the article's title. A word of warning: Copying graphics can be tricky until you get the hang of it. You may decide the results are more reliable if you import the same graphic in a new position. In the meantime, remember the Undo button!

1. With the graphic selected, click the Copy button.

2. Click an insertion point at the beginning of the second paragraph, and click the Paste button. Word inserts a copy of the graphic in its frame at the insertion point.

3. Move the pointer to the right side of the pasted graphic, where you think the invisible frame is. When a four-headed arrow appears below the pointer, hold down the left mouse button, and drag a dotted outline of the frame to the right end of the article's title. When you release the mouse button, the graphic appears in the new location of its frame.

4. With the second graphic still selected, choose Frame from the Format menu. Set the Horizontal Position to *6.75* (so that the graphic sits 6.75 inches from the left edge of the page) and the Vertical Position to *0.5*, and click OK.

5. Now all that's left to do is rebreak the flyer's title for a more balanced effect. Click an insertion point before the *f* of *for*, and press Shift+Enter. Turn the page to see the results.

Turning off graphics display

Inserting graphics in a document can slow down the rate at which you can scroll through the text. To increase the scrolling speed, choose Options from the Tools menu, click the View tab, click Picture Placeholders in the Show section, and then click OK. Word substitutes placeholders for the graphics. Reverse this procedure to turn on graphics display.

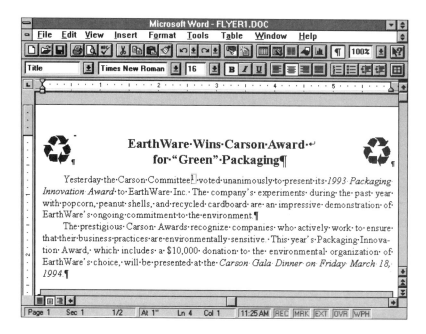

6. If your printer can handle graphics, print the flyer. Then save it by clicking the Save button.

Creating Tables

Tables provide visual summaries of information and enable us to quickly grasp relationships that might be lost in narrative explanations. Creating tables in Word for Windows is a simple process. You specify the number of columns and rows and then leave it to Word to figure out the initial settings.

To demonstrate how easy the process is, we'll add a table to the flyer:

Jumping to a specific page

If your document has several pages, you can use the Go To command on the Edit menu to jump to a specific page. Choose Go To, enter the page number, and click the Go To button. You can also jump directly to specific sections and lines, and to elements such as footnotes, graphics, and tables.

1. Press Alt+Ctrl+PageDown to move to the top of the flyer's second page.

2. Save a new version of the document as FLYER2.DOC.

3. Click the Insert Table button to drop down a column/row grid.

4. Drag the pointer across four columns and down six rows. The grid expands as you drag beyond its bottom edge, and Word shows the size of the selection below the grid. When you release the mouse button, Word inserts this table structure in the document:

Cell　　　　　　*Cell marker*

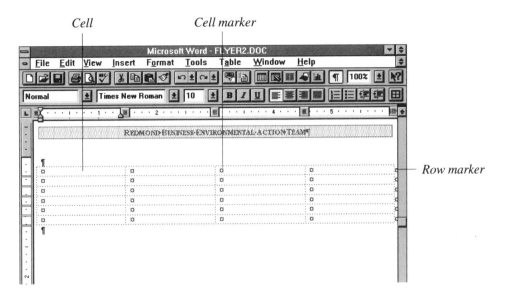

— *Row marker*

As you can see, Word has created a table with four equal columns that together span the width of your document's text column. The insertion point is in the first *cell* (the intersection of the first column and the first row). To make an entry in this cell, all you have to do is type, like this:

Cells

1. To enter column headings, type *Contributor* in the first cell, and press Tab. The insertion point moves to the cell to the right. Type *Sulfur Dioxide*, and press Tab to move to the next cell. Type *Carbon Monoxide*, and press Tab. Finally, type *Nitrogen Oxides*, and press Tab. Here's the result so far:

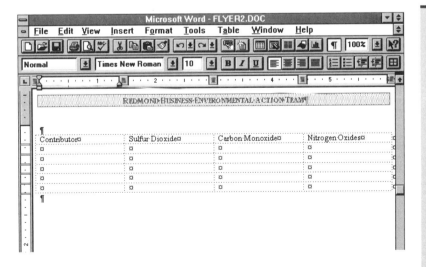

More control over table creation

You can create a table with specific column widths by choosing the Insert Table command from the Table menu and entering the table specifications in the Insert Table dialog box. From this dialog box, you can also start the Table Wizard, which guides you through the process of creating a table with one of six predefined formats. See Chapter 3 for more information about wizards.

Pressing Tab at the end of the first row moved the insertion point to the first cell in the second row.

2. Finish the table by typing the entries shown below, pressing Tab to move from cell to cell. (Pressing Shift+Tab moves the insertion point to the previous cell, and you can also use the Arrow keys and mouse to move around.)

Transportation	*0.9*	*41.2*	*8.1*
Industrial Emissions	*3.4*	*4.7*	*0.6*
Fuel Combustion	*16.4*	*7.6*	*10.8*
Solid-Waste Burning	*--*	*1.7*	*0.1*
Miscellaneous	*--*	*6.0*	*0.2*

Looking over the table, you can see one or two changes that would make it more effective. We discuss ways to edit tables in the next section.

Rearranging Tables

You can rearrange the rows and columns in a table in much the same way that you rearrange text. Follow these steps to move the *Carbon Monoxide* column to the left of the *Sulfur Dioxide* column:

Moving a column

1. First move the pointer above the third column and, when the pointer changes to a downward-pointing arrow, click the mouse button to select the column.

2. Hold down the mouse button, and drag the shadow insertion point to the beginning of the *Sulfur Dioxide* heading. Release the mouse button to move the *Carbon Monoxide* column to the left of the *Sulfur Dioxide* column, as shown here:

Commands for selecting

If you have trouble selecting parts of a table with the mouse, you can use the Select Row, Select Column, and Select Table commands on the Table menu.

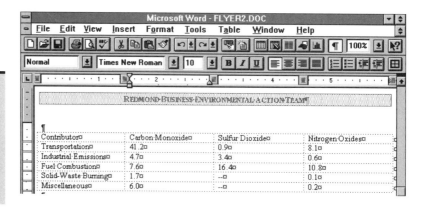

You can use any of the editing techniques we've described for ordinary text with tables, so feel free to experiment.

Changing Column Width

You can adjust column widths in three ways: by moving the markers designated with grids on the ruler, by dragging column borders, or by using the Cell Height And Width command. Follow these steps to change the widths of the columns in the example table:

1. With the insertion point located anywhere in the table, move the pointer over the marker to the left of the first column on the ruler. The pointer changes to a two-headed arrow. Drag to the right until the 1-inch mark is exposed in the gray part of the ruler. Word moves the table over by 1 inch.

   Changing the left indent

2. Next drag the column marker between the first and second columns to the 1.5-inch mark on the ruler, and then drag the column marker between the second and third columns back to the 2.25-inch mark. Word adjusts the widths of the first and second columns to reflect these changes.

   Changing column widths with the ruler

3. Now adjust the third and fourth columns using a different method. First point to the dotted vertical column border to the right of the third column, and then drag the two-headed pointer to the left so that *Sulfur Dioxide* breaks neatly on two lines. Repeat this procedure for the fourth column. Here are the results:

   Dragging column borders

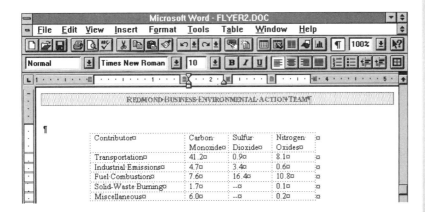

The headings in the second, third, and fourth columns wrapped to two lines because Word's default row-height

Deleting rows and columns

To delete one or more rows or columns, select the rows or columns, and choose Delete Rows or Delete Columns from the Table menu. (If you don't select rows or columns first, the command is named Delete Cells, and choosing this command displays a dialog box in which you can specify what you want to delete.) To delete the entire table, select the table, and then choose the Delete Rows command.

setting is Auto, meaning that Word wraps long entries to the number of lines needed to display the entries in their entirety, adjusting the height of the row as necessary. If you want all entries to appear on only one line, select the table, choose Cell Height And Width from the Table menu, select Exactly from the Height Of Rows drop-down list, specify an At setting that is a couple of points larger than the font size used in the table (for example, 12 pt if the font size is 10 pt), and click OK.

Adding a Title

Suppose you want to add a row above the table to contain a title. The first step is to insert a new row:

1. Move the pointer into the selection bar adjacent to the first row of the table, and click to select the entire row.

Inserting rows

2. Choose Insert Rows from the Table menu. Word inserts the number of rows you have selected—in this case, one.

Next, you need to join the cells of the new row to create one large cell to accommodate the table's title. Joining cells is a simple procedure, as you'll see if you follow these steps:

Joining cells

1. With the first row of the table selected, choose Merge Cells from the Table menu. Word merges the cells into one large cell that spans the table.

2. Now finish the task by entering the title. Click an insertion point in the top row, type *AIR POLLUTANT SOURCES*, press Enter, and type *In Millions of Metric Tons*. Your table now sports a new title:

New rows shortcut

You can quickly insert blank rows in a table by selecting the number of rows you want to insert and then clicking the Insert Rows button on the toolbar. (The Insert Table button becomes the Insert Rows button when you are working in a table.) Word inserts the new rows above the selection. You can add new rows to the end of a table by placing the insertion point just before the end-of-cell marker in the last cell and pressing the Tab key.

Formatting Tables

Having made all the necessary structural changes to the table, let's add some finishing touches. First, we'll format the title and headings:

1. Select the first two rows of the table, and click the Center button.

2. To make the title and headings in the *Contributor* column bold, point to the grid line above the title, click to select the title row and the first column, and then click the Bold button. (Although the cell containing the title spans all four columns, Word considers it to be the first cell in the first column.)

Well that was simple. Now let's see how to decimal-align the numbers in the second, third, and fourth columns. This involves setting decimal tabs in each of these columns. Follow the steps below:

1. Click the Tab button at the left end of the ruler until it is set to a decimal tab (an upside-down *T* with a period).

2. To align the numbers in the *Carbon Monoxide* column on the decimal point, drag through the five cells containing numbers in that column to select them, and then click the 2 mark on the ruler to set a decimal tab where you want the decimal points to line up.

3. Repeat the previous step to decimal-align the *Sulfur Dioxide* and *Nitrogen Oxides* numbers in about the middle of their columns. The table now looks like this:

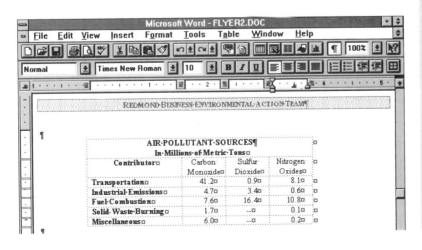

Setting tabs

By default, Word sets tab stops at half-inch intervals across the page. You can set custom tabs in two ways: using the ruler and using the Tabs command. To use the ruler, click the Tab button at the left end of the ruler until it displays the type of tab you want (left, center, right, or decimal), and then click the ruler where you want a custom tab. The tab takes effect for the paragraph containing the insertion point or selected paragraphs only. To remove a custom tab, point to it, and drag it away from the ruler. To set a custom tab with the Tabs command, choose Tabs from the Format menu, and specify the tab in the Tabs dialog box. You can clear selected tabs or all tabs in this dialog box, and you can specify that the tabs should have leader characters such as dots or dashes.

Before we wrap up this section, let's add grid lines to the cells and put a border around the whole table:

1. With the insertion point anywhere in the table, choose Select Table from the Table menu. Then choose Borders And Shading from the Format menu to display this dialog box:

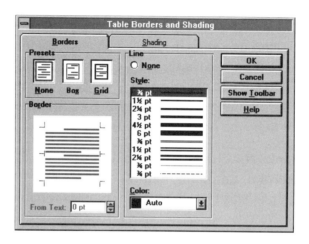

Adding grid lines and borders

2. In the Presets section, click Grid. In the Line section, select the 1 1/2 pt double line as the Style setting, and click OK.

Now use another method to add a double line under the title:

1. Click anywhere in the title row, and click the Borders button on the Formatting toolbar.

2. Click the down arrow to the right of the Line Style box, and select the 1 1/2 pt double line. Then click the Bottom Border button. Here are the results:

Turning off grid lines

The grid lines that form the cell boundaries of a table don't print, but they can help you visualize the structure of the table. To get an idea of how the table will look when printed, choose Gridlines from the Table menu to turn off the grid lines. Choose the command again to turn them back on.

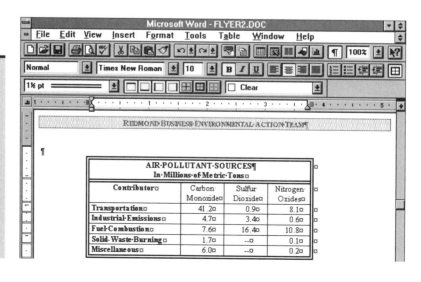

3. Now hide the Borders toolbar by clicking its button again, and save your work.

Adding Formulas

Later in this chapter, we demonstrate how to import a spreadsheet into Word, but Word 6 for Windows includes a variety of spreadsheet functions that you can use to build formulas directly in Word tables. You saw examples of a couple of formulas at work in Chapter 3 in the Invoice template, which automatically calculated merchandise costs, subtotals, and a grand total when you entered the quantity and unit price of an invoice item. Let's add a total row to the pollutants table and see how easily you can turn a Word table into a spreadsheet. Here are the steps:

1. Start by adding a row to the bottom of the table. Click an insertion point between the table's right border and the last row marker, and press Enter.

Adding a row for totals

2. In the first column of the new row, type *TOTAL*, and then press Tab to move to the next column.

3. Choose Formula from the Table menu to display the dialog box shown here:

Using the SUM formula

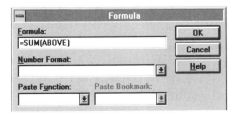

As you can see, Word has entered =SUM(ABOVE) in the Formula edit box, meaning that it assumes you want to add together the numbers in the cells above the active cell and put this total in the active cell.

4. Click OK, and press Tab to move to the next column.

5. Choose Formula from the Table menu again. This time, the Formula edit box contains =SUM(LEFT) because the cell to the left of the active cell contains a number and the cell above contains text (--). Select the word *LEFT*, type *ABOVE*, click OK, and then press Tab.

Putting text beside a table

To put text adjacent to a table, switch to page layout view, insert a frame adjacent to the table, and click an insertion point in the frame. Then type and format your text as usual. Word wraps the text within the frame, which you can size and position as needed (see page 123).

6. Choose Formula from the Table menu, and click OK to accept the default formula. The table now looks like this:

Let's see how to average the pollutants:

Turning a table into tabular text and vice versa

To convert a table to tabular text, first choose Select Table from the Table menu to select the entire table, and then choose the Convert Table To Text command from the Table menu. Indicate how you want Word to separate the information now in columns, and click OK. Word removes the table grid and separates the text that was in columns as you indicated. To turn a block of regular text separated by tabs into a table, select all the tabular text, and click the Insert Table button on the toolbar. If the text is separated by characters other than tabs, select the text, choose Convert Text To Table from the Table menu, indicate the number of columns and how the information is separated, and then click OK.

1. Add a row to the bottom of the table, type *AVERAGE* in the first column of the new row, and press Tab.

2. Choose Formula from the Table menu, double-click the Formula edit box, and press Delete to erase the default entry.

3. Type an = sign, and then click the down arrow to the right of the Paste Function edit box to display a list of functions. Click AVERAGE. Word pastes the function and a set of parentheses in the Formula edit box.

4. The numbers you want to average are in the second column—column B—and in rows 3 through 7 of the table, so type *B3:B7* between the parentheses, and click OK.

5. Repeat steps 2 through 4 for the other two columns, using C3:C7 and D3:D7 as the cell specifications.

You might want to take some time to explore Word's functions on your own. They may not let you create sophisticated stock projections or loan analyses, but if your spreadsheet formulas usually involve nothing more complex than a few mathematical calculations, being able to create spreadsheets within Word may save you considerable time.

Creating Charts

Word for Windows allows you to cut or copy charts and graphs from other applications and then paste them into a Word document. But the Word 6 for Windows package also includes Microsoft Graph, a charting program with which you can create charts based on information in your Word document. Let's briefly explore this capability using part of the table you just completed. Follow these steps:

1. Click an insertion point below the table, and press Enter to add some space.

2. Using the mouse in the selection bar, select rows two through seven of the table (in other words, select everything but the title, total, and average rows), and click the Copy button. Then click the Insert Chart button on the toolbar. After a pause, your screen looks like this:

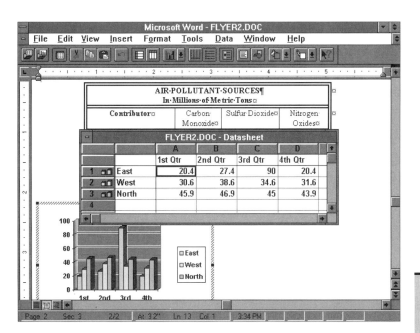

3. In the Datasheet window, click the gray square in the top-left corner to select all the cells, and press Delete.

4. Next click the top-left highlighted cell, and choose Paste from the Edit menu. The data from the pollutants table is pasted into the datasheet.

No table in your document?

If you want to include a chart in your document but not its table of data, you can enter the data in the datasheet that appears when you click the Insert Chart button on the toolbar. As you enter your data in the datasheet, watch as the chart changes to reflect the data.

5. Click the chart. The Datasheet window disappears.

Not a bad beginning, but the chart obviously needs some adjustments. Follow these steps:

1. To plot the data by column instead of by row, choose Series In Columns from the Data menu.

2. To change the 3D column chart (vertical) to a 2D bar chart (horizontal), click the arrow to the right of the Chart Type button to display these chart formats:

3. Click the second format in the first column (the 2D bar chart format).

Enlarging the chart window

4. So that all the labels on the vertical axis can be displayed, let's make the chart window a little bigger. Move the pointer over the bottom-right corner of the chart window until it changes to a two-headed arrow. Then drag the border to the right until all the labels fit neatly.

5. Now let's add a title. Choose Titles from the Insert menu, select the Chart Title option, and click OK to attach a title to the chart. Then drag through the word *Title*, type *AIR POL-LUTANT SOURCES*, press Enter, and type *In Millions of Metric Tons*.

6. If some of the labels have disappeared, drag the top of the chart frame upward to resize the chart.

Importing charts

You can import and edit an existing Excel chart in Microsoft Graph as long as the chart is saved in its own file. Simply click the Import Chart button on Graph's toolbar, select the file, and click OK. To import a chart created in Lotus 1-2-3, select the datasheet, click the Import Data button on the toolbar, select the file, and click OK.

With these adjustments completed, you can close Graph and update the chart in FLYER2.DOC:

1. Click anywhere outside the chart frame.

   That's all there is to it. When you return to your document window, the chart has been inserted at the insertion point, below the table. Now we can make a few more adjustments:

1. Scroll the window until you can see the two paragraph marks below the chart. Then move the pointer over the chart, and click to select it. Hold down the mouse button, drag the shadow insertion point to the left of the first paragraph mark, and release the mouse button. The chart moves down.

2. Next choose Borders And Shading from the Format menu, select Box in the Presets section and the 1 1/2 pt double line as the Style setting in the Line section, and click OK.

   Adding a border to the chart

3. Choose Paragraph from the Format menu and set a left indent to nudge the chart into aesthetic alignment with the table. (A Left setting of 0.78 does the job.) Here are the results:

4. Click the Save button to safeguard your work.

To edit a chart, simply double-click it to return to Graph. You can then reformat the chart and change its type.

Although Microsoft Graph doesn't offer all the capabilities of dedicated charting programs, you will often find that it is all you need to quickly generate visual representations of your data. You might want to spend a little more time experimenting with this program, using the simple table we have created in this chapter or more complex sets of your own data.

Importing Spreadsheets

As you've seen, Word allows you to create impressive tables and do some mathematics with ease. However, it can't calculate complex formulas and functions the way a spreadsheet program can. And although a spreadsheet program is great for performing calculations, it lacks the word-processing capabilities you need to put together dynamic reports. Suppose you have gone to a lot of trouble to create a spreadsheet and you want to include the spreadsheet's data in a report. It would be frustrating to have to rekey all that information into a Word table for presentation. Fortunately, you don't have to. With Word 6 for Windows, you can combine the best of both worlds—the numeric know-how of a spreadsheet program with the word-processing proficiency of Word.

To demonstrate, we'll import this spreadsheet, which was created with Microsoft Excel for Windows:

Supported spreadsheet and database formats

At present, files from the programs listed below can be imported into Word for Windows documents:

Microsoft Excel for Windows versions 2.x, 3.0, 4.0, and 5.0

Lotus 1-2-3 releases 2.x and 3.x

Microsoft Access

Microsoft FoxPro

dBASE

Paradox

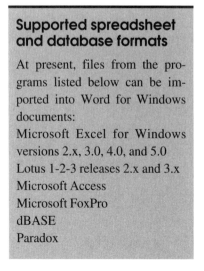

To import an Excel file, you can click the Insert Microsoft Excel Worksheet button on the toolbar. However, you might want to import spreadsheets that were created in other programs, so we'll show you the most generic method. Follow these steps with your own spreadsheet file:

1. Press Ctrl+End to move to the end of the flyer, and press Enter to insert a blank line and give yourself some room to move.

2. Choose File from the Insert menu. Word displays the File dialog box.

3. From the List Files Of Type drop-down list, select All Files (*.*). In the Directories list, select the directory in which the spreadsheet is stored. Then in the File Name list, double-click the spreadsheet file you want to import. If the spreadsheet file contains multiple sheets, you must also identify which sheet you want to use. Word then displays this dialog box, in which you specify whether you want to import the entire spreadsheet or only a range:

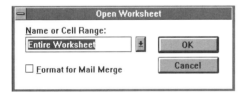

4. Either accept the default Entire Worksheet option, or type the range you want to import. Then click OK to start the conversion process. When Word finishes the conversion, the spreadsheet file is inserted as a table at the insertion point.

You can edit the spreadsheet table using the techniques described earlier. The printout of FLYER2.DOC at the beginning of the chapter shows the demonstration spreadsheet after we made a few cosmetic adjustments.

By itself, Word for Windows can create some pretty fancy documents. Add a few graphics, tables, and charts, and you've got documents with real distinction! So be adventurous, and let Word help you generate documents that will make your clients and colleagues sit up and take notice.

Embedding/linking data from other applications

You can create a dynamic link between spreadsheet or database information and a Word document either by embedding the information as an object in the Word document or by linking the information in the source file to the Word document. The embedding technique involves choosing Object from the Insert menu, and either selecting the file, clicking Link To File, and clicking OK; or selecting the program in which you want to create the object, entering the object's information in the source application, and then embedding it in the Word document. The linking technique involves opening the information in the source application, copying it to the Clipboard, switching to the Word document, choosing the Paste Special command from the Edit menu, clicking Paste Link and specifying the type of link, and then clicking OK. If the linked information changes, you can update the information in the Word document by choosing the Links command from the Edit menu. (Note that in order to create a link between Word and another application, you must be running both applications.)

6

Mail Merge:
Creating Form Letters and Labels

What you will learn...

Felix Katz
Symbiotics, Inc.
12834 NE 91st Street
Redmond, WA 98052

Dear Felix:

Thank you for your
Styrofoam packagin
growth of our organ

Sincerely,

Ted Lee

Harry Dawg
Synergy Unlimited
15 Central Way
Redmond, WA 98052

Dear Harry:

Thank you for your
Styrofoam packagin
growth of our organi

Sincerely,

Ted Lee

Hugh Manatee
Apex Productions
14320 NE 21st Street
Redmond, WA 98052

Dear Hugh:

Thank you for your generous contribution of $150 to our fund to construct a facility for the recycling of Styrofoam packaging material into potting soil. We are very excited about this project, which will help the growth of our organization, as well as that of numerous potted plants.

Because Apex Productions has demonstrated such an ongoing commitment to Redmond BEAT over the past year, the board would like to invite you to add your company's name to our list of corporate sponsors. Enclosed is more information.

Again, thank you.

Sincerely,

Ted Lee

Felix Katz
Symbiotics, Inc.
12834 NE 91st Street
Redmond, WA 98052

Most people in the United States have received at least a few personalized form letters. Even kids get them! You know the sort of thing—your name is sprinkled liberally throughout, with a few references to the city in which you live or some other item of personal information. Mail of this sort is an example of the use, and often the abuse, of the Mail Merge feature available with many word-processing programs. We certainly don't want to assist in the destruction of the forests of the world by showing you how to send junk mail to millions of people. But if you'll use your new knowledge wisely and with restraint, we'll introduce you to the mysteries of mail merge.

Actually, with Word for Windows, mail merge isn't even all that mysterious. If you have used this feature in other word processors or in previous versions of Word, you'll be pleasantly surprised at the ease with which you can now create mail merge documents using Word for Windows. For those of you who have never used mail merge (or *print merge*, as it is often called), we'll start with a definition.

What Is Mail Merge?

Mail merge is the printing of a bunch of similar documents by merging the information in one document, called the *main document*, with what is essentially a database of variable information in a second document, called the *data source*.

The main document

The main document contains the information that does not change from document to document—the text of a form letter, for example—along with placeholders called *merge fields* for the variable information and codes that control the merging process. A main document with a typical set of codes is shown at the top of the next page.

Merge fields

The data source

Each word enclosed in chevrons is a name that matches the name of a field in the corresponding data source, also shown on the next page. As you can see, the data source contains the information that changes with each printed document: first name, last name, company, address, and so on. The data in this particular document is stored in a Word table, but you can

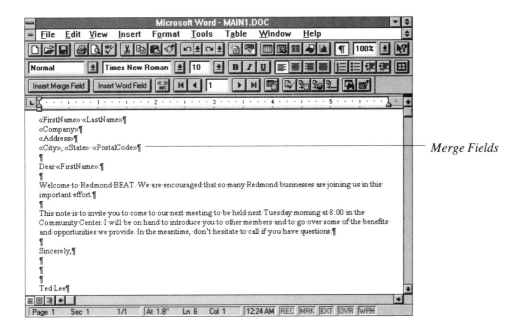

Merge Fields

Field name   *Field*

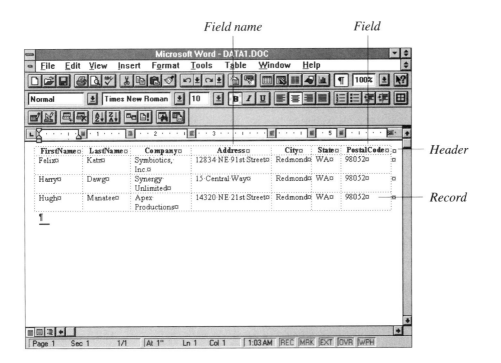

Header

Record

use other formats. (Called *tab-delimited fields* or *comma-delimited fields*, these formats are standard output formats for most spreadsheets and databases.) In the table, each row, which is called a *record*, contains the variable information for

Records

Fields

Headers and field names

one printed document. Each cell (the intersection of a column and a row), which is called a *field*, contains one variable item, usually a single word or a short phrase. You can include as many records as you want (or as many as disk space permits) in a data source. When using the table format, you can have up to 31 fields per record. (With other formats, the number of fields is practically unlimited.) The first record (the top row of the table) is called the *header*. Each field in the header contains a *field name* that identifies the contents of the column below it.

As you'll see later in the chapter, the result of merging the sample main document and data source shown on the previous page is three letters, each with the appropriate information instead of the merge fields. Although mail merge documents can be pretty complex—they can include mathematical calculations, logical comparisons, and branching instructions—most are as simple as the sample documents we'll use in this chapter.

In addition to creating letters, mail merge is a handy tool for filling in forms and is particularly useful when the information needed to fill in the forms is already included in a database or spreadsheet. For example, you might use mail merge to print invoices, checks, and insurance forms, as well as all kinds of labels—for mailings and for collections of disks, audio cassettes, CDs, video tapes, and books. Printing labels of various types is such a common use of mail merge that Word for Windows includes instructions to guide you through the process. We'll have a look at labels in a moment. Right now, let's create the sample form letter.

Creating Form Letters

The first stage of creating a form letter is to take a few moments to plan it. You might draft a sample letter and mark all the words or phrases that will vary from letter to letter. Then you might organize your sources of information to make sure you have easy access to all the names, addresses, and other tidbits of information required. Only after these tasks have been completed will you actually create the main document

Field location

The location of the fields in the data document is not important to the operation of the Print Merge command. The main document can use any combination of fields in any order. If the order of fields is significant to you, you can insert them manually or move them after they have been inserted.

and data source. Assume that we have already taken care of this planning stage for you so that you can now start the interesting part.

Creating the Main Document

To set up your main document, follow these steps:

1. Click the New button to open a new document. (In actual practice, you might base the letter document on a letterhead template or some other template, but for this example, the document can be based on the default Normal template.)

2. Click the Save button, and in the Save As dialog box, assign the name MAIN1.DOC to the file, and click OK. If you want, go ahead and fill out a document summary.

3. Choose Mail Merge from the Tools menu to display the dialog box shown here:

Starting mail merge

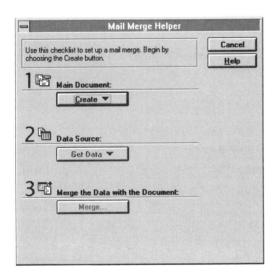

As you can see, Word is ready to lead you through the mail merge process.

4. Follow the suggestion at the top of the dialog box and click the Create button. A list drops down, offering you the choices shown on the next page.

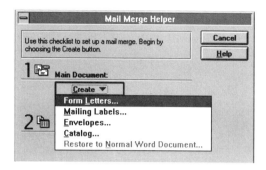

5. Select Form Letters. Word displays this dialog box:

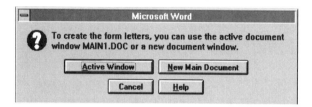

6. Click the Active Window button to use MAIN1.DOC as your main document.

Now let's create the data source, which will contain all the variable information for the form letters.

Creating the Data Source

With most word processors, you have to create the data source before you begin the mail merge process. With Word, you can either open an existing data source or have Word guide you through the procedure for creating one, like this:

Creating a new main document

You don't have to create the main document before you begin the mail merge operation. After selecting Form Letters from the Create list, you can click the New Main Document button to create a new blank document based on the Normal template that you can later use as the basis for the main document.

1. With the Mail Merge Helper dialog box still open, click the Get Data button to drop down this list of options:

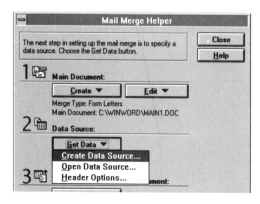

2. Select Create Data Source to display this dialog box, which helps you set up the fields of your data source:

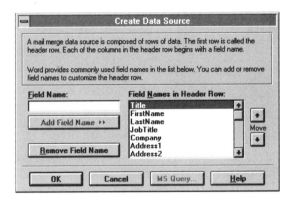

3. The list box on the right displays commonly used field names. You want this data source to have FirstName, LastName, Company, Address, City, State, and PostalCode (ZIP) fields. You don't want the selected field name, Title, so click Remove Field Name to remove it from the list. Also remove JobTitle, Address2, Country, HomePhone, and WorkPhone.

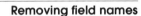

Removing field names

4. Now remove Address1 from the list, and then with Address1 in the Field Name edit box, delete the 1, and click Add Field Name to add Address back to the list.

Editing field names

5. With Address still selected, click the Move up arrow repeatedly to move the Address field up until it is between Company and City. The dialog box now looks like this:

Rearranging field names

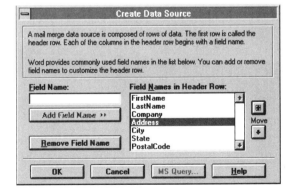

6. Click OK to close the dialog box. Word displays a Save Data Source dialog box (similar to the Save As dialog box) so that you can provide a name for your new data source.

Field name rules

Field names can have as many as 40 characters and can include letters, numbers, and underscore characters. Each field name must start with a letter and cannot contain spaces. To get around the "no spaces" rule, you can assign multiword fields names, such as LastName or LAST_NAME.

7. Assign the name DATA1.DOC to the document, and click OK. Word displays this dialog box:

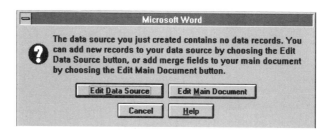

8. Click Edit Data Source to display the following dialog box, where you can begin entering records in the data source:

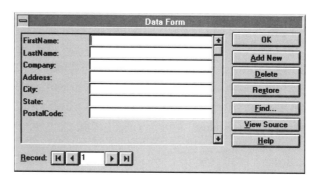

9. Go ahead and enter the information shown here:

Field	Record1	Record2	Record3
FirstName	Felix	Harry	Hugh
LastName	Katz	Dawg	Manatee
Company	Symbiotics, Inc.	Synergy Unlimited	Apex Productions
Address	12834 NE 91st Street	15 Central Way	14320 NE 21st Street
City	Redmond	Redmond	Redmond
State	WA	WA	WA
PostalCode	98052	98052	98052

10. Press either Tab or Enter to move from field to field. After you fill in the last field in one record, click the Add New button to move to a new record. You can use the arrows at the bottom of the screen to move back and forth through the records.

11. After entering the three records, click OK. Word closes the dialog box and returns you to the main document.

Completing the Main Document

When you return to the main document, the most obvious change is the addition of a Mail Merge toolbar between the Formatting toolbar and the ruler. This toolbar makes it easy to add placeholders for the variable information that will be merged from the data source. You might want to move the pointer over the buttons on the Mail Merge toolbar, checking out their names and descriptions.

The Mail Merge toolbar

The next task is to type the text of the letter, inserting merge field placeholders. Let's start by entering the addressee information, which consists almost entirely of merge fields:

1. With the insertion point at the top of the blank document, click the Insert Merge Field button on the Mail Merge toolbar to drop down a list of the available fields.

Inserting merge fields

2. Click FirstName. The FirstName merge field appears at the insertion point, enclosed in chevrons. (If Word displays {MERGEFIELD FirstName} instead of «FirstName», press Alt+F9 to turn off the display of codes and turn on the display of merge fields. If Word displays the actual first name from your first record, click the View Merged Data button on the Mail Merge toolbar to display the merge field.)

Displaying merge fields

3. Press the Spacebar, click the Insert Merge Field button again, click LastName to insert the LastName merge field, and then

Using an existing data source

If you want to use an existing Word document as the data source for your form letters, select Open Data Source from the Get Data list in the Mail Merge Helper dialog box, and then select the file you want to use. (The information in the file must be set up in a table or be separated by tabs or commas for Word to be able to use it as a mail merge data source.) You can also use existing database information from other applications as the data source. Candidates are databases created in certain versions of Microsoft Access, Microsoft Excel, Microsoft FoxPro, Paradox, Lotus 1-2-3, and WordPerfect. The process for opening a database created in another application is basically the same as that for opening a Word document, although a file conversion program (supplied with Word) is often needed to complete the task.

Formatting merge fields

You can format merge fields the same way you format any text. Simply select the fields, and use the buttons on the Formatting toolbar or the character formatting options in the Font dialog box. Then when Word merges the main document and the data source, it applies the formatting specified in the main document to all the merged documents.

press Enter to start a new line. Insert the Company merge field, and press Enter. Repeat this procedure for the Address merge field.

4. Click Insert Merge Field, insert City, type a comma and a space, insert State, type two spaces, and insert PostalCode.

5. Press Enter a couple of times, and then type *Dear* and a space.

6. Insert the FirstName merge field, type a colon (:), and press Enter twice.

7. Now type the body of the letter, as shown here:

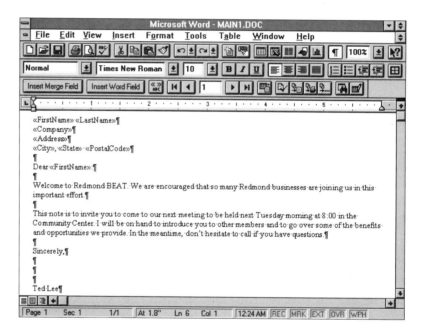

8. Save the document.

Merging the Documents

You are now ready to merge the main document with the data source. You have several options here. Notice the set of four buttons toward the right end of the Mail Merge toolbar. If you click the Check For Errors button, Word checks that your main document and data source are set up correctly. If you click the Merge To New Document button, Word merges the main document with the data source and puts the resulting letters in a new document that you can save and print later. If you click the Merge To Printer button, Word merges the main document and data source but sends them directly to the printer. If you click the Mail Merge button, Word displays a dialog box in which you can specify where to merge the records, which records to merge, whether blank fields are to be printed, and so on.

Specifying mail merge options

1. Click the Check For Errors button to display these options:

Checking for errors

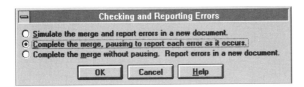

2. Select the Simulate option, and click OK. If you followed our instructions, you should see a dialog box announcing that Word found no mail merge errors. (Word points out any errors so that you can correct them.) Click OK to return to your document.

Merging to a new document

3. Now click the Merge To New Document button. Word opens a new document window called *Form Letters1* and then "prints" the letters to the document, with a section break between each letter, like this:

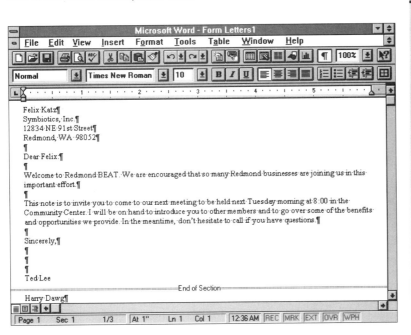

4. Close Form Letters1, saving it when prompted with the name FORM1.DOC (the default).

Merging selected records

If your data source contains many records and you want to merge only those records that meet certain criteria (for example, only those with specific ZIP codes), you can "filter" the records to extract the ones you want. The filtering process is too complex to discuss thoroughly here, but basically, you click the Query Options button in the Mail Merge Helper dialog box and specify your criteria on the Filter Records tab. For example, setting Postal-Code equal to 98052 filters out for merging all the records in the data source with 98052 in the Postal-Code field.

5. If your printer is turned on and you want to try the Merge To Printer button, go ahead and click it, and then click OK in the Print dialog box. Your printed letters will look like those shown at the beginning of the chapter.

Now that you know how to do simple mail merges, let's look at some more sophisticated mail merge capabilities.

Creating More Sophisticated Letters

We named the main document and data source for this example MAIN1.DOC and DATA1.DOC, respectively, but we could have saved them with any valid names. And we can open and edit the documents just like any other documents. The data source is just a normal document that contains a table, so we can add fields and records to this table the same way we can add columns and rows to any table. And we can add tables, charts, pictures, and various types of Word fields to the main document. We can even include fields that cause the mail merge process to pause and prompt for additional information that is not included in the data source.

Word gives you several methods of controlling exactly what is printed in a merged document. Although these methods are not very complicated, a complete explanation of them is beyond the scope of this book. However, we can quickly turn our original form letter into one that makes a decision about what to print, just to give you an idea of what can be done.

Adding Fields to the Data Source

Let's create a letter thanking people for their contributions to Redmond BEAT, and include a paragraph that Word prints only if the contribution is over a certain amount. To allow Word to make the printing decision, we have to add a field to the data source to hold the amount of the contribution. Follow these steps:

1. Because DATA1.DOC is just another Word document, click the Open button on the Standard toolbar, select the filename, and click OK to open the file in a window on top of the main document. Word displays the Database toolbar between the Formatting toolbar and the ruler in the data source's window.

Catalogs

When you want to create lists of information using the fields in a data source, select the Catalog option from the main document's Create list in the Mail Merge Helper dialog box. For example, suppose your company wants to create a list of employee names and emergency phone numbers using three fields from a personnel database. After selecting Catalog and identifying the data source, you enter the LastName, FirstName, and EmergencyPhone fields once in the main document. When you click the Merge To New Document button, Word creates one document containing the specified information for all the employees in the data source.

2. Click the Manage Fields button on the Database toolbar to display this dialog box:

3. Type *Contribution* as the field name, and press Enter. Word adds the field to the bottom of the list and the right end of the table. Click OK to close the dialog box.

4. If necessary, adjust the width of the *Contribution* column in the table so that the field name fits on one line.

5. Credit each of the people in your data source with a contribution. Make one for $50, one for $100, and one for $150.

6. Click the Mail Merge Main Document button on the Database toolbar to move back to the open main document.

Returning to the main document

Editing the Main Document

Instead of creating a new main document from scratch, we'll edit the one we've already saved. Here's how:

1. Select the two paragraphs between the salutation and the closing, and delete them.

2. Now type the following:

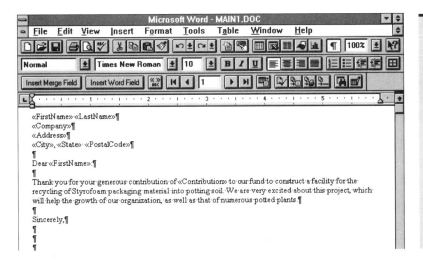

Adding data to the data source

After creating a new field in the data source, you can add the field information in two ways: You can type the information directly in the data source table; or you can click the Data Form button on the Database toolbar to display the Data Form dialog box, where you can add the field information to each record in turn.

Inserting a new merge field

When you get to the contribution, click the Insert Merge Field button, and select the new Contribution field. Then finish the paragraph, but don't press Enter.

Next we need to enter the conditional statement that will control printing of an additional paragraph based on the amount of the contribution. Here goes:

Inserting a conditional statement

1. With the insertion point at the end of the first paragraph, type a space. Then click the Insert Word Field button to drop down a list of fields, and select the If...Then...Else... option. Word displays this dialog box:

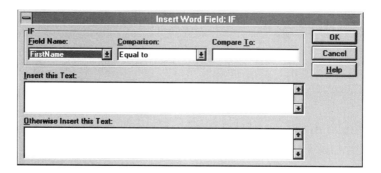

2. Click the arrow to the right of the Field Name edit box to drop down a list of field names. Scroll down to Contribution, and click it to insert it in the Field Name edit box.

Using comparison operators

3. Drop down the Comparison list, and select Greater Than.

4. Click the Compare To edit box, and type *100*.

5. Press Tab to move to the Insert This Text box, and type *Text If True*.

6. Press Tab to move to the Otherwise Insert This Text box, and type *Text If Not True*.

Turning on field codes display

7. Click OK to close the dialog box, and then press Alt+F9 to turn off the display of merge fields and turn on the display of field codes, which look like this:

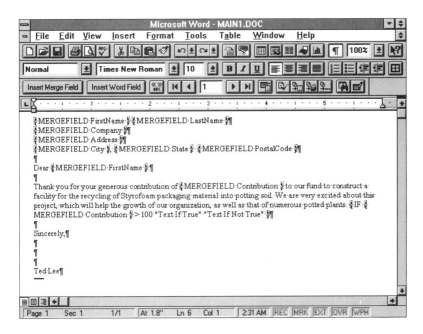

You have just inserted a conditional statement that tells Word to print *Text If True* if the value of the contribution is greater than $100 and to print *Text If Not True* if the contribution is not greater than $100. You obviously don't want to actually print *Text If True* and *Text If Not True*, but it's easier to set up the conditional statement this way and then replace *Text If True* and *Text If Not True* in the field code with the real text. Here's how:

1. Select the three words *Text If True* (but not the quotation marks enclosing them), and press Enter twice to start a new paragraph. Then type the following, inserting the Company merge field where indicated:

   Because {MERGEFIELD Company} *has demonstrated such an ongoing commitment to Redmond BEAT over the past year, the board would like to invite you to add your company's name to our list of corporate sponsors. Enclosed is more information.*

   Press Enter twice.

2. Next select *Text If Not True*, and delete it, leaving the two quotation marks surrounding nothing (""). Now if the contribution is not greater than $100, Word will print nothing.

Adding text to the conditional statement

3. Finally, click an insertion point to the left of the paragraph mark at the end of the conditional statement, and type *Again, thank you.* (be sure to include the period). The main document now looks like this:

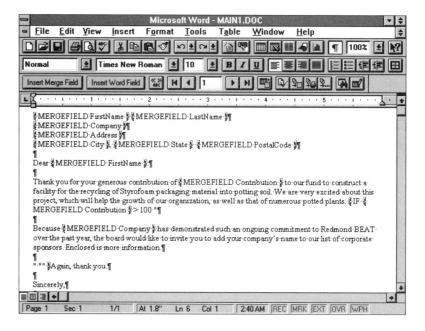

4. Save the main document as MAIN2.DOC.

That's all there is to it. You now have several options to check the results of your efforts. You can click one of the buttons on the Mail Merge toolbar to merge the letters to a document or to the printer, or you can look at the results right in the main document. Try this:

Viewing the merged data

1. Press Alt+F9 to turn off the field codes, and then click the View Merged Data button on the Mail Merge toolbar to display the data from the first record in place of the merge fields.

Cycling through records

2. Click the right and left arrows on the Mail Merge toolbar to cycle through the records in your data source. (The current record number is displayed in the box between the arrows.) Here's the merged data for the third record, which has a contribution of $150:

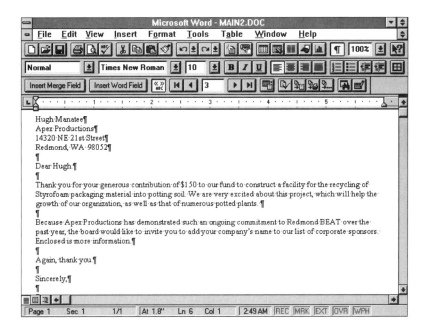

3. If you credited the three companies with contributions of $50, $100, and $150, the first two letters don't have the extra paragraph and the third letter does. Try changing the comparison operator from > to >= (greater than or equal) by pressing Alt+F9 to display the field codes, clicking an insertion point after the >, and typing an equal sign. Then press Alt+F9 again, and cycle through the records to see the result.

Changing the comparison operator

4. Save the main document and data source, and then close all open documents to prepare for the next example.

Now let's take a look at how the Mail Merge feature can help you print labels.

Creating Labels

When you used the Mail Merge Helper dialog box to create a form letter, you undoubtedly noticed that it could also be used to create labels and envelopes. In this section, we discuss the procedure for printing multiple labels. (If you want to print just one label or envelope, use the Envelopes And Labels command on the Tools menu, as described in the adjacent tip.) The procedure for printing multiple envelopes is similar to the one we'll describe here; if anything, you'll find that printing envelopes is easier because you have fewer options to deal with.

One envelope or label

If you want to print a single envelope or label, choose Envelopes And Labels from the Tools menu. You can then click the tab for either Envelopes or Labels in the resulting dialog box. Click Options to change the envelope or label size; fill in any variable information; and then click Print to print the envelope or label.

Follow these steps to create a set of mailing labels for the sample form letter:

1. Click the New button on the toolbar to create a new document that you can use as the main document for your labels.

2. Choose Mail Merge from the Tools menu to display the Mail Merge Helper dialog box shown earlier on page 143.

3. Click the Create button in the Main Document section, and select Mailing Labels from the list of options. When Word asks whether you want to use the active window or create a new document, click Active Window.

4. Back in the Mail Merge Helper dialog box, click the Get Data button in the Data Source section, select Open Data Source from the list of options, and double-click DATA1.DOC in the Open Data Source dialog box.

Selecting a label

5. Word advises that you now need to create the main document. Click Set Up Main Document to display this dialog box, which helps you define the label you want to use:

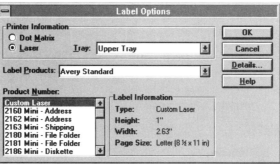

Notice that you can select either Dot Matrix or Laser in the Printer Information section. Word uses this setting to determine the type of labels displayed in the Product Number list: Laser labels typically come on 8-by-11-inch sheets, and dot matrix labels come on fanfold paper.

Other types of labels

In addition to regular address labels, Word can print labels for shipping, file folders, name tags, disks, audio and video tapes, and several types of cards. It is worth exploring whether Word can help automate some of your routine label-making tasks.

6. Scroll through the Product Number list to get an idea of what is available. (You can highlight an item to see general information about it in the adjacent Label Information section. Click the Details button to see more information about the selected label.)

7. Select the 5161 Address label if you have a laser printer or the 4143 Address label if you have a dot matrix printer. Click Details. This dialog box appears for the 5161 Address label:

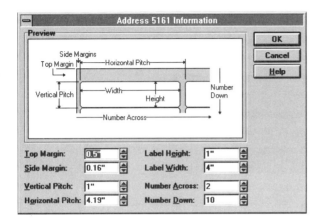

As you can see, the Information dialog box displays a drawing of the selected label, with its characteristics listed below. You can change each characteristic—margins, pitch, height, width, and number across and down—by entering a new value in the corresponding edit box. This flexibility is handy if you want to print labels in a format that isn't included in Word's lists. You can select a format that is similar and then fine-tune it in the Information dialog box.

8. Go ahead and change the characteristics of this label, and watch the drawing change. Then click Cancel to close the dialog box without recording your changes.

9. Click OK to close the Label Options dialog box. Word displays this dialog box so that you can create the label format for your main document:

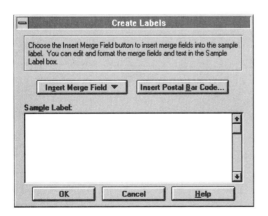

Inserting merge fields in
the label

10. Create the label format the same way you created the addressee portion of the form letter earlier in the chapter. Click the Insert Merge Field button, select FirstName, press the Spacebar, click Insert Merge Field, select LastName, and press Enter. Then insert the Company, Address, City, State, and PostalCode merge fields, like this:

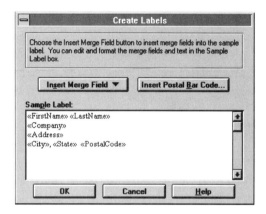

Be sure the bottom line of the label text consists of the three merge fields shown above, with punctuation and spacing included.

11. Click OK to return to the Mail Merge Helper dialog box, and then click Merge in the Merge The Data With The Document section to display this dialog box:

Adding bar codes

You can cut down on postage costs for bulk mailings by printing a POSTNET bar code on your labels or envelopes. To insert a bar code, click the Insert Postal Bar Code button in the Create Labels dialog box, select the fields that contain the ZIP code and street address (or post office box number), and click OK. Word prints the bar code at the top of the label (or above the address on an envelope).

12. Click Merge to merge the labels to a new document rather than the printer. After a couple of seconds, you should see something like this on your screen:

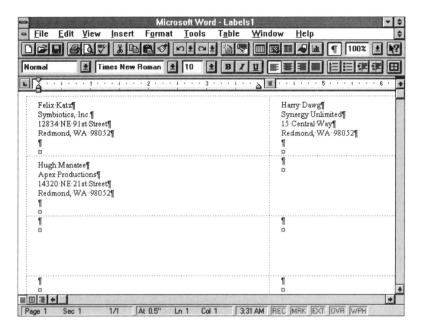

13. If you want, save the merged document with a name such as the default LABEL1.DOC so that you can print it later. Save the main document with a name such as LBL_MAIN.DOC so that you can reuse it in the future.

That's all there is to it.

You might want to test-print the labels on plain paper to check their alignment, and then you can replace the paper with label sheets and print away! After you have been through the process a once or twice, you will probably find that it takes you less time to merge a batch of labels than it did to read these instructions. And printing a batch of envelopes is even easier: Just select Envelopes from the list that drops down when you click the Create button in the Main Document section of the Mail Merge Helper dialog box, and follow Word's instructions. You can create a default return address for your envelopes by choosing Envelopes And Labels from the Tools menu, entering a return address in the Return Address box on the Envelopes tab, and clicking Add To Document. When Word asks if you want to save the return address as the default, click Yes.

Index